'*Space, Place and Territory* makes a valuable contribution to our understanding of the processes of urbanization. It is equally adept in describing the qualities of the built environment as it is the conceptual tools that bring about its transformation.'

Mohsen Mostafavi, Dean and Alexander
and Victoria Wiley Professor of Design,
Harvard Graduate School of Design, USA

'In this book Fábio Duarte makes a novel and important contribution to the understanding of the core concepts of space, place and territory in urban studies. The core problematic USPT addresses is the distinctive uniqueness of each concept whilst simultaneously exploring the complex interdependencies between them. Creatively empirical analyses of sensing, mapping, conceiving and contesting the city USPT builds and populates the metaphor of the spatial matrix – a novel framework for analyzing how society is profoundly shaped by spatial features.'

Professor Simon Marvin, Director of the Urban
Institute University of Sheffield, UK

Space, Place and Territory

Space, place and territory are concepts that lie at the core of geography and urban planning, environmental studies and sociology. Although space, place and territory are indeed polysemic and polemic, they have particular characteristics that distinguish them from each other. They are interdependent but not interchangeable, and the differences between them explain how we simultaneously perceive, conceive and design multiple spatialities.

After drawing the conceptual framework of space, place and territory, the book initially explores how we sense space in the most visceral ways, and how the overlay of meanings attached to the sensorial characteristics of space change the way we perceive it – smell, spatial experiences using electroencephalography, and the changing meaning of darkness are discussed. The book continues exploring cartographic mapping not as a final outcome, but rather as an epistemological tool, an instrument of inquiry. It follows on how particular ideas of space, place and territory are embedded in specific urban proposals, from Brasília to the Berlin Wall, airports and infiltration of digital technologies in our daily life.

The book concludes by focusing on spatial practices that challenge the status quo of how we perceive and understand urban spaces, from famous artists to anonymous interventions by *traceurs* and hackers of urban technologies. Combining space, place and territory as distinctive but interdependent concepts into an epistemological matrix may help us to understand contemporary phenomena and live them critically.

Fábio Duarte is scholar and research lead at the Massachusetts Institute of Technology – Senseable City Lab, and professor at the Pontifícia Universidade Católica, Curitiba, Brazil.

Space, Place and Territory
A Critical Review on Spatialities

Fábio Duarte

LONDON AND NEW YORK

First published 2017
by Routledge
2 Park Square, Milton Park, Abingdon, Oxon OX14 4RN

and by Routledge
711 Third Avenue, New York, NY 10017

First issued in paperback 2018

Routledge is an imprint of the Taylor & Francis Group, an informa business

© 2017 Fábio Duarte

The right of Fábio Duarte to be identified as author of this
work has been asserted by him in accordance with Sections 77 and 78 of
the Copyright, Designs and Patents Act 1988.

All rights reserved. No part of this book may be reprinted or
reproduced or utilised in any form or by any electronic, mechanical,
or other means, now known or hereafter invented, including photocopying
and recording, or in any information storage or retrieval system,
without permission in writing from the publishers.

Trademark notice: Product or corporate names may be trademarks
or registered trademarks, and are used only for identification
and explanation without intent to infringe.

British Library Cataloguing-in-Publication Data
A catalogue record for this book is available from the British Library

Library of Congress Cataloguing in Publication Data
A catalog reference for this book has been requested.

ISBN 13: 978-1-138-34205-7 (pbk)
ISBN 13: 978-1-4724-8379-9 (hbk)

Typeset in Sabon
by Florence Production Ltd, Stoodleigh, Devon, UK

This book is dedicated to Roti Turin
(*in memoriam*)

and to Vanessa and Valentina

Contents

Acknowledgements   xi

1   Introduction   1

2   Constructions   11

The construction of space   11
The construction of place   29
The construction of territory   44

3   The enactment of space, place and territory   63

Space/Space   64
Space/Territory   66
Territory/Territory   67
Territory/Place   71
Place/Place   74
Space/Place   75

4   Sensing the city   79

Smelling space, smell-space   80
Brain spaces: measuring brain activity in urban
    environments   84
Sensing the night   87

5   Mapping the city   99

6   Conceiving the city   115

Brasília: the construction of an idea   115

7 Conceiving the city: what is next? 129

Adding, carving, weaving 129
The Berlin Wall 135

8 Challenging the city 149

9 Final remarks: spatial negotiations 161

Index 165

Acknowledgements

In 2002 I published *Crise das matrizes espaciais* in Brazil (published by Perspectiva). This book was a first attempt to define space, place and territory as singular but mutually formative concepts. I also argued that they form spatial matrices upon which we can analyze human relations with each other and with the world. Although published by a renowned publisher and well-received by readers, the book was written in Portuguese, which meant it had a relative small scholarly audience. I would like to thank the Universidade de São Paulo, Brazil, the Université Laval, Canada and the Université Paris I, institutions where I spent three years doing research and writing *Crise das matrizes espaciais*.

Since then, I have been testing these ideas in lectures, classes and conversations with colleagues, as well as revisiting these concepts with the help of new books and scholarly papers, widening the range of authors and disciplines, acknowledging the limitations of my initial work, as well as its strengths. The first part of this present book owes much to this initial publication and the intellectual process it has triggered. Key ideas and a few examples were maintained in the present book; otherwise, most of the text has been changed, concepts were polished, and examples added and refined in order to make my arguments clearer.

For almost 15 years, I have enjoyed a vivacious research environment in the Graduate Program in Urban Management at the Pontifícia Universidade Católica do Paraná, Brazil. Among my dear and intellectually energizing colleagues, Rodrigo Firmino has been a friend and a prolific and challenging co-author, with whom I have discussed many of the concepts presented here, and who gave valuable suggestions. Vanessa Sevilhano, my wife, read some of the chapters and gave me good advice on how to make them friendlier to readers. I could not have written this book without the stimulating environment I encountered over the last 3 years at the Massachusetts Institute of Technology. Its rich libraries, and the mix of brilliance and openness with which ideas are debated among students and faculty, helped me to critically review my manuscript. I am specially grateful to my colleagues at the Senseable City Lab, with whom I have discussed some of the ideas presented here.

1 Introduction

> ... il n'y a pas un espace, un bel espace, un bel espace alentour, un bel espace tout autour de nous, il y a plein de petits bouts d'espace, et l'un de ces bouts est un couloir de métropolitain, et un autre de ces bouts est un jardin public; un autre (ici, tout de suite, on entre dans des espaces beaucoup plus particularisés), de taille plutôt modeste à l'origine, a atteint des dimensions assez colossales et est devenu Paris, cependant qu'n espace voisin, pas forcément moins doué au départ, s'est contenté de rester Pontoise.
>
> (Georges Perec (2000) *Espèces d'espaces*. Paris: Galilée, p. 14–15 © 1974)

Space, place and territory are concepts that lie at the core of disciplines such as geography and urban studies. Despite or perhaps because of this, such concepts are both polysemic and polemic. However, although space, place and territory are indeed polysemic and polemic, they have particular characteristics that distinguish them from each other, making them unique. They are interdependent concepts, but not interchangeable. They share the same conceptual substratum, but the differences between them explain how we simultaneously perceive, conceive and relate with multiple spatialities. Therefore, the conceptual and methodological approach proposed in this book aims to maintain the balance between a common conceptual core and the uniqueness of each term.

There are other 'spatial' terms that have deep-rooted conceptual lineages which have been employed to understand the relationships between humans and their surroundings. These include land, terrain, region, landscape and a few others. They are neither more nor less important than the concepts discussed in this book. However, these concepts are more closely tied to specific disciplines. Region is frequently discussed in geography, economics and sociology, but is seldom mentioned in architecture or urban design – and when it is mentioned, it is either as a *fait accompli* or as a concept derived exactly from geographic, economic or sociological work. Landscape,

2 Introduction

on the other hand, is an important topic for architecture, urban planning and urban design, but is rarely discussed in economics or sociology with the same scholarly conceptual accuracy as region, or for that matter, space, place and territory.

In this book I argue that space, place and territory are the key concepts that form the spatial matrices with which we can analyze how humans establish relations with each other and with the world, namely their physical and social surroundings.

Even though authors have been acknowledging the importance of each term, projects that make an effort to simultaneously embrace, differentiate and relate them are rare. Yi-Fu Tuan is an exception because of his profound and extensive oeuvre covering two of these concepts: space and place – although not much territory, and sometimes dealing with them interchangeably, which might hamper the analysis of some spatial phenomena. More recently, scholars have published in-depth studies of each concept individually, shedding new light on the definition of each term and their roles in understanding contemporary events. Authors such as Edward Casey, Stuart Elden and Rob Shield offer in-depth studies on place, territory and space. Although they do see commonalities and relations between these concepts, these analyses often deal with one or a pair of these concepts, and sometimes treat them as if they were opposites. If this strategy might help to make one concept clearer, it diminishes or does not take advantage of the complementarities that exist between them.

In his insightful work defining place and indicating its conceptual relevance and independence from other similar concepts, Edward Casey mostly builds his arguments by discussing the importance of place in relation to time, or almost a counterpoint to space. Casey (1993: 288) argues 'the dual dominance of Space and Time is an expression, as well as an original and continuing cause, of the neglect of Place in human experience.' His books not only focus *on* place, but also advocate *for* place in a world dominated by long narratives built upon space and time. As I discuss further on, this is a common feature of theories of place, which often mix conceptual and political worldviews, aiming to promote place before other ontological concepts.

Stuart Elden acknowledges Casey's efforts to present a historical account of the concept of place, and himself adopts a similar incumbency focusing on territory. Elden stresses the crux of the concept of territory as the political features which establish power relations over portions of space. On one occasion, Elden (2013: 17) points out that '[t]erritory is not simply an object: the outcome of actions conducted toward it or some previously supposedly neutral area. Territory is itself a process, made and remade, shaped and shaping, active and reactive.' I fully agree with Elden,

Introduction 3

and I add that the same is true for space and place. And as I discuss in this book, as processes that involve sensorial, cultural and social aspects, a portion of space is not a territory in itself, but becomes a territory depending on how it is appropriated by a certain group, and how the values impinged over this portion of space direct the way those who occupy it must behave. One difference that becomes clear between the literature on place and territory is that often the former focuses on affects, and the latter on politics. Where there is an evident advocacy in the literature related to place, there is political criticism underpinning the literature on territory.

It is generally accepted that space is the baseline of any other spatial concept, and there is extensive scholarly literature on space. Two recent examples in English come from Doreen Massey and Rob Shields, both of whom rely on the work of Henri Lefebvre, a key author on space as a social and political construction. The social and political aspect of Lefebvre's approach to space is the focus for the great majority of authors dedicated to the theoretical treatment of space, from Manuel Castells to Neil Brenner. But there is another body of literature, exemplified by a recent book by Shields (2013), that aims to combine multispectral approaches on the definition of space, ranging from sociology and philosophy to mathematics and astronomy. Yet as with other books on space, other spatial concepts are seldom mentioned. And on the rare occasions when they are mentioned, they do not receive the same careful conceptual treatment.

In all these accounts, the authors continue an important lineage of scholars seeking a balance between philosophical inquiry and everyday experience in the discussion of space, place and territory. This lineage includes authors as varied as Martin Heidegger and Milton Santos, Yi-Fu Tuan and Gaston Bachelard. The main strength of each of these books is an in-depth theoretical discussion of each term, stressing that the concepts of space, place and territory have been transformed throughout history, according to different temporalities within different disciplines. The downside of most of them, though, is that they commonly focus only on one of the terms. In the rare cases where the other concepts are mentioned, either a certain philosophical advocacy emerges, implicitly or explicitly giving prevalence to one of the concepts over the others, or space, place and territory are treated as synonyms (which they are not). As a consequence, similar phenomena are exclusively analyzed in some of these books through one specific conceptual lens. Although this strategy helps to refine each concept individually, it flattens the complex conceptual relief that these phenomena have. Space, place or territory do not yield inherent or unchangeable characteristics, but rather are defined through the relationships we establish with portions of spaces according to individual and social values.

4 *Introduction*

In this book I discuss that the use of multispectral lenses that combine space, place and territory without making them interchangeable may bring different perspectives to the study of spatial phenomena. Additionally, in this book I give special attention to urban phenomena.

In order to define space, place and territory as particular concepts sharing common features, I begin the book with a chapter entitled *Constructions*. Here I present the conceptual construction of these three terms, stressing their common roots but also their uniqueness as well as their interdependence. Space is the substratum of all the other concepts, but must not be confused with any of them. Space is simultaneously the most immediately perceived of the concepts discussed here and the most abstract. Space is visceral and cerebral at the same time; we feel space before we rationalize it, but in order to explain it, we need well-defined, clear and singular concepts. Place and territory have space as their substratum, and both are portions of space to which we attribute personal or social values. But while place is defined by affective values, territory tends to be demarcated through imposed values; while place is chiselled by subjective values, territory tends to reign over those who occupy it. The goal of this chapter is to mark the singularity of each concept, and at the same time make it clear that they share core features.

Space, place and territory are interdependent but not interchangeable. They are related to each other in such deep senses that they can coexist harmoniously or acrimoniously in the same portion of space. I pro-pose to discuss these relationships between space, place and territory as spatial matrices. In this chapter, I pair up the concepts and explore what happens when they occur simultaneously in the same portion of space. Space and place, space and territory, place and territory, and also space and space, place and place, and territory and territory form the spatial matrices. Sometimes one does not interfere in the existence of the other, sometimes their mutual existence is reciprocally beneficial, and sometimes coexis-tence triggers conflicts that often lead to the elimination of one form of spatial appropriation by another.

Constructions and matrices form the conceptual core of this book. Both mix theoretical inquiries with examples selected with the intention of illustrating the arguments. Once the conceptual ground is established, the book enters a second portion, divided into four sections. Although concepts of space, place and territory are crucial to different geographic scales and disciplines, in this book I mostly focus on one particular phenomenon: the city. City is defined as the material manifestation of a multi-scalar and cross-disciplinary phenomenon which is equally dependent and transforms the natural environment, scientific-and-technological artefacts, and social arrangements.

In the chapter *Sensing the city*, I explore how we sense space in the most visceral ways, but also how the overlay of meanings attached to the sensorial characteristics of space change the way we perceive it. I begin this chapter by exploring smell. Smell has not been codified, and is arguably the sense that yields the most profound and involuntary memories of space. Like an olfactory *madeleine*, a particular smell can remind us of spaces and spatial experiences, but the opposite is not true. Think of a portion of space: you probably can envision it, but not recall its smells. Our olfactory memory is as volatile as smells themselves. But once we smell something, the recollection of a particular situation or space is powerful. Smell has been mostly removed from our daily urban experience, the same has happened with other sensorial phenomena, such as complete darkness or touch. Our lives and cities are becoming bland-scapes. A myriad of smells were omnipresent in cities. Smells did not carry moral values, and functioned simply as distinctive characteristics of portions of spaces. Today, there are good and bad smells – and preferably, for shared spaces, no smells. However, as recent as the early twentieth century, cities were still full of odours and neighbourhoods were recognizable by their smells. True, in a bland-scape, it is easy to draw a romantic picture of a rich and complex landscape of smells. The fact is that the urban smell-scape encompassed untreated wastewater, trash in the streets, slaughterhouses and factories near houses, and vehicles burning fossil fuels. For these reasons, it is not uncommon to see connections drawn between unpleasant smells (the definition of which is also contentious) and poverty and specific ethnicities, which are often grouped in specific areas of cities, strengthening the correlation between smells and social prejudices.

Smell has a long history of overlapping meanings, showing how sensorial and cultural filters influence each other. In this sense, visceral experiences of space are rapidly influenced by cultural values. When we describe how we sense space, another layer of meaning is superimposed: we have to interpret these experiences, which inevitably involve other cultural layers such as language. I continue the chapter on *Sensing the city* by looking at research that analyzes brain activity in different spatial experiences, paying special attention to electroen-cephalography (EEG). This technology is not better than others at exploring how spatial experience is reflected in brain activity, but researchers have been using portable EEG devices to map brain activity in real time, creating cycles where the user responds directly to his or her spatial experience based on how the brain processes space.

I finish this chapter highlighting how a sensorial aspect of the urban environment has been impregnated with cultural values: the night. What happens to space in complete darkness? Whether describing or concept-

6   *Introduction*

ualizing space, we usually take for granted that we see space. However, even for sighted people, darkness is a common experience and affects spatial perception. Darkness influences how people sense space, not only by changing one's perceptual sensibilities – when sight is impaired, people use other senses – but also by the meanings that darkness has acquired throughout history. And night is the natural empire of darkness. Nevertheless, the connotations of night have changed throughout history, along with the ways in which people deal with the spatial characteristics of darkness. In Medieval Europe, night had conflicting meanings: it was either seen as the realm of God, symbolizing the world before creation ('And God said, Let there be light: and there was light'), or the realm of the devil and witchcraft in the late-Middle Ages. Modernity and electrification of streetlights have brightened the night to the point of eliminating complete darkness. I finish this essay by discussing how the lack of darkness and changes in the meaning of night influence our perception and understanding of space.

Mapping the city deals with one form of representing space, place and territory: maps. As any other representation, maps are profoundly ideological, and are also affected by the available scientific knowledge and technological tools. But my interest in this chapter lies not so much in maps as outcomes of processes of representing portions of space, but in the mapping process itself. As a highly descriptive tool, mapping deals primarily with including all features of space. However, the representation of any object or phenomenon necessarily involves deciding which features to select and which features to leave out. Different methodologies have intentionally or implicitly favoured certain features, which consequently influence the way we perceive and conceive space, place and territory. In this chapter, I explore mapping as an epistemological tool; cartographic mapping not as a final outcome, but rather as an instrument of inquiry. Maps are not passive representations of reality, but mapping is an active way of investigating the multiple dimensions of space, place and territory. Maps attempt to convey new spatial understandings of the world, and also serve as social and political tools, such as the navigational maps used during the golden age of European navigation. Maps can also operate as a territorial technology aimed at reinforcing particular worldviews, such as world maps based on the clear limits of nation-states, which do not have any relation to geographical features. But mapping can also be instrumental to unveil the vibrant urban lives that are hidden under traditional maps of the city, such as cognitive or mental maps. More recently, locative and mobile devices are pushing the boundaries of mapping as an ephemeral and dynamic look at the urban phenomenon on both the micro and macro scales, from mapping individual use of the city to correlating urban flows on a global scale, flows that naturally vanish on a daily basis, appearing and disappearing in different cities. The analysis of mapmaking, which is also entrenched with technological, social, cultural and political values, sheds light on how entities and flows are perceived and organized as they are filtered by sensorial and cultural filters.

The chapters on sensing and mapping the city help us to discuss how the concepts of space, place and territory are marked by sensorial and cultural filters, and how they are interdependent though singular; how space, place and territory have epistemological as well as political uses. In both cases, the baseline question of *'what is . . .'* is supported by the existence of a certain space, place and territory. In the chapter *Conceiving the city*, I focus on what the city could be, and how particular ideas of space, place and territory are embedded in specific urban proposals. There is a long history of city plans as the materialization of how spatial features would advance proposals to change social, economic and formal aspects of urban life. Brasília is the constructed synthesis of how modern spatialities should be, and how this ideal space would reflect and foster an emergent modern society. When Brasília was inaugurated in 1960, the supreme modernist approach of an ideal space encompassing and fostering universal values had been harshly criticized, and other planning methodologies were emerging. Yet Brasília's groundbreaking combination of aesthetically powerful urban design and architecture is a cornerstone of any reflection on how spaces, places and territories emerge from a virtually untouched terrain. Brasília was not an attempt to create new possible spatialities, but an urban and architectural statement about what a city should be. For this reason, any essay on Brasília is risky, for this city is a concretization of a dogma. And yet when real life starts to permeate the modernist city, unexpected places and territories emerge.

Derived from the least creative part of the modernist canon, land-use planning based on the definition of functional zones with strict construction parameters became a mantra which is still practiced and taught around the world. This form of bureaucratic and authoritative planning divides the city into precise territories, and neglects the emergence of spontaneous spaces and places which gives life to the city. However, while zoning has pervaded the least-inspiring realms of urban design, experimentation has been a constant for planners. Experimentation feeds the way we analyze present cities, and the way we envision the future of cities. Indeed, only 10 years after the inauguration of Brasília, Peter Cook (1970: 14) stated that he saw the 'emergence of a truly international "underground" or network', and gave examples of architects and urbanists proposing ephemeral infrastructures, portable cities, and the use of telecommunications and early computers as components of future cities.

8   *Introduction*

Fifty years after the climax and inevitable decline of the ideal modernist space, 50 years which saw a mix of bureaucratic planning and provocative urban design experimentations combining underground and networked approaches, the design of cities as a way of indirectly changing society is still engrained in architectural and planning practices on different scales. In the second part of *Conceiving the city*, I propose to understand the construction of spaces, places and territories that underlies contemporary urban proposals. The construction of the wall dividing Berlin during the Cold War is a pivotal element in urban design, although it is barely recognized among urban designers. The wall is a territorial device *par excellence*, but was also iconic of spatial elements that were shaping urban life throughout Europe, and the meaning of the wall to eastern and western Berliners involved different ways of constructing place in the city, during and after its existence. I continue by discussing airports. Rather than an example of a meaningless place, whose historical and social distance from local values make them the epitome of a *non-place*, I argue that airports may be quite the opposite: the *über-place* of the contemporary global space. Finally, I discuss the infiltration of digital technologies in the urban space. Since McLuhan's insightful and stimulating ideas that media was at the core of social transformations (and not any particular content), communication technologies would connect the whole world in a global village, and computation would ultimately change the way we think, several urban scholars and designers have been debating similar ideas. For some, information and communication technologies efface space; for others, they give rise to globally unified spaces; and for others, a network of places exchanging information is the future of global urban spaces.

In the final chapter before the final remarks, I focus on spatial practices that challenge the status quo of how we perceive and understand urban spaces. Artworks play a major role questioning how we perceive, conceive and understand space, place and territory. These may range from well-known artists to anonymous interventions. Conspicuous artists have shown how artefacts may play a subversive role in cities. Christo and Jeanne-Claude have been proposing large-scale interventions that question preconceived ideas we have regarding which elements are part of the urban and regional spaces, and how they should be arranged. By wrapping bridges, buildings, promenades and islands with synthetic fabric, Christo and Jeanne-Claude make us aware of our blindness towards them. They highlight their physical qualities by temporarily suppressing their symbolic values. By wrapping up the *Pont Neuf*, in Paris, Christo and Jeanne-Claude stifle its historical and ornamental symbolisms, turning it into a sculpture – but rather than carving the stone, he covers it. But at the same time he muffles the bridge's symbolisms –

Introduction 9

which daily users do not really pay attention to – the artist highlight them through a sense of loss: what if these symbolisms were removed from this portion of space, would this space be the same even if the physical element of the bridge were still there? Krzysztof Wodiczko's interventions are even subtler: they last only a couple of days or hours, and do not leave any trace – somehow, they do not even touch the city. Wodiczko projects steady images and films onto monuments and buildings. Aware of the territorial symbolisms that some of these elements have, by conveyed particular social and cultural values, Wodiczko choose provocative topics related to these values. But tense relations emerge, such as when live testimonies of immigrants and low-paid labourers are projected onto the façade of a museum in San Diego facing the United States. Wodiczko challenges the natural and uncritical integration of such monuments and symbolic buildings into the daily life of a city.

Besides these well-known artists, equally important are anonymous figures like skateboarders and practitioners of parkour (*traceurs*), who use the materiality of the city to question the cultural values embedded within it, or media artists who hack surveillance cameras to expose how daily life is controlled through territorializing technologies. This chapter aims to show that there is an ongoing movement to challenge the concepts of space, place and territory before they crystallize, and to remind us that their conceptual power lies precisely in their malleability and continuous transformation.

I conclude briefly reminding key ideas discussed throughout the book, and argue that spatial matrix, intertwining space, place and territory, may be a methodological tool to shed light in cultural conflicts, environmental crisis and technological changes. Indeed, these topics provoke cyclical and deep spatial transformations. But claiming they create *non-places*, provoke deterritorialization, or produce virtual spaces detached from our daily experience give only momentary intellectual help. Moment passed, here we are, in space: living space, discussing space. Combining space, place and territory as distinctive but interdependent concepts into an epistemological matrix may help us to understand such phenomena and live them critically.

2 Constructions

The construction of space

Being in space is a primal condition of our existence. A wide range of scholars – including philosophers, physicists, geographers, architects, sociologists – have for centuries discussed the importance of space in human existence. Yet there is still no single, clear and consensual definition of space. Societal changes transform our understanding of space – from the primacy and pervasiveness of the Catholic religion in all aspects of life in the European Middle Ages to the conceptual and technological breakthroughs of science, which have marked modern western society, paradigm shifts have occurred in our understanding of the world and how space is perceived and conceived. Space has not just been multiple throughout history, though. At any point in time, people perceive and conceive space differently, on both individual and collective levels. Yet it is not enough to say the concept of space is multiple. As both a mental and sensory experience that is vital for human existence, it is legitimate to keep asking basic questions: how can space be defined? Is there a universal formative logic of space, to which all known or yet-to-be-discovered spaces would be subject? If space is plural – ranging from oneiric to economic spaces, how can such plurality be embraced under the concept of space?

When Timaeus describes the world, with the creation of the stars, the soul, the elements and time, he stresses that first the intellect was placed in the soul, then the soul in the body, followed by the formation of the Cosmos, which therefore came from the soul and the intellect (Plato, 2003). When Timaeus spoke of what existed before the act of creation he used the term Khôra, which would be the formless receptacle that fed the world, because it is

> formless, and free from the impress of any of those shapes which it is hereafter to receive from without. For if the matter were like any

12 *Constructions*

> of the supervening forms, then whenever any opposite or entirely different nature was stamped upon its surface, it would take the impression badly, because it would intrude its own shape. Wherefore, that which is to receive all forms should have no form . . .
>
> (Plato, 2003: 214)

Jacques Derrida (1993) writes that it is the interpretations of Khôra that give it form, depositing 'the sediment of their contribution', without exhausting interpretations or forms. Derrida's brief essay singles out the impossibility of naming it, defining its *physis* and *dynamis* and questioning even the possibility of discussing them. For Derrida (1993: 25), Khôra 'does not have the characteristics of an intelligible or sensible existent. There is Khôra but the Khôra does not exist'. This receptacle of possibles is prior to the creation of any element, and even of space. Things and beings exist through it, while it withdraws itself. In a balance between being and becoming, Khôra can only be apprehended when it gives form, and existence, to others. Edward Casey (1993: 359) writes that Khôra is a precosmic stage, and existence occurs when it takes place through Khôra, which, despite being formless, functions as a 'participational and topological matrix onto which the Demiurge can superimpose the geometric shapes from which solid objects are built up in a cosmic architecture'. Building on the concept of Khôra, we could say that rather than being something pure or absolute, space is constructed at the exact moment it allows the formation of beings, things and flows.

Space as a primal condition of our existence encompasses physical and subjective aspects. Martin Heidegger (1971: 179) states that space is where 'Earth and Sky, Gods and Mortals' acquire unity: 'The simple oneness of the four we call *the fourfold*. Mortals *are* in the fourfold by *dwelling*.' Several authors have highlighted Heidegger's contribution to the discussion of space. For Stuart Elden (2001), Heidegger has shown 'the site, the place of poetic dwelling (. . .) is the truth of being.' Mike Crang (2005: 205) posits 'there is no unplaced knowledge, no transcendent viewing point and no unplaced transcendent subject'; and for Otto Bollnow (2001: 24), also building on Heidegger, 'There is space only insofar as man is a spatial being, that is, a being that forms space and, as it were, spreads out space around itself.' Human beings are spatial not because our body occupies a position in space, but because our existence is conditioned in relation to surrounding entities and flows; and space brings these elements into existence, and is formed by them.

There is a classic distinction between Newton and Leibniz's definitions of space. For Newton, space is absolute, an entity in itself, containing objects and events that are dependent on space to come to life. On the other hand, Leibniz's definition of space is relational; its existence depends on the interactions between objects and events. In Leibnizian terms space 'has no powers independent of objects and events but can be construed only from the relations between them' (Agnew, 2012: 83). One of Leibiniz's phrases has been quoted extensively since its first publication in 1715 for those studying space: as 'something purely relative, like time space being an order of co-existences as time is an order of successions' (1995 © 1715). Recently, Manuel Castells (2014) said that 'Not being a German philosopher, I simplified it: space is the material support of simultaneity' – exactly the same as what Foucault (1986: 22) had said forty years earlier: 'We are in the epoch of simultaneity: we are in the epoch of juxtaposition, the epoch of the near and far, of the side-by-side, of the dispersed.' However, this simultaneity also produced the postmodern aesthetic of pastiche, and hinders the notion that space is equally shaped by what will happen, or what might happen, or what we wish to happen. Likewise, the present is a singularity that vanishes instantaneously as it happens, but also a combination of different temporalities coming together: of short and long cycles – daily routines, festivals and life events – of sacred and profane temporalities (Crang, 2012).

On the one hand, space is not simply relative, but relational: a 'product of interrelations; as constituted through interactions, from the immensity of the global to the intimately tiny' (Massey, 2005: 9). On the other hand, the 'differing sense of space of different epochs is not just a story about accuracy of measurement, it is about differing societies' relationship with space' (Crang, 2012: 203). As mentioned previously, the understanding and use of space change throughout history and across different cultures and distinct temporalities. The malleability of space is not just a philosophical characteristic, but is actually perceived in distinct temporal and spatial scales throughout history.

Rob Shields presents a history of theories of space ranging from mathematics to sociology, and shows that 'advances in understandings of space and spatialisation advance and retreat, are proclaimed and lost for centuries' (Shields, 2013: 41). Still, a definition cannot simply state that space is relative and relational. Intellectual inquiry needs to begin with a tentative definition. Let me begin by highlighting a few recent attempts to define space.

Doreen Massey (2005) seeks a definition of space which encompasses the 'association between the spatial and the fixation of meaning' and another, more 'mobile, flexible, open, lively'. A concise characterization of space comes from another recipient of the Vautrin Lud prize – considered the most important award in geography. Milton Santos (1979; 1990) defines space as a set of fixed elements and flows, with the former coalescing flows that consequently redefined the fixed elements. Santos

14 *Constructions*

(1990) also defined space as the relationship between systems of objects and systems of actions. Objects are non-human, natural and man-made constituents of space; actions, on the other hand, are always human, since, for Santos, actions must have an end, an objective – while action in nature is 'blind, with no future'. Santos argues that in nature things simply exist, they are not created or produced. This notion is central for Henri Lefebvre's (1981) definition of social space, which always involves objects produced by humans. Lefebvre also differentiates between object and product, in which the former is unique and irreplaceable, while the latter is made so that it can be repeated endlessly both as a concrete piece as well as the social acts that produce it. Nature enters into both authors' concept of space, but it is a signified nature, nature introduced by humans in their system of objects and actions.

A key feature of Lefebvre's and Santos's definitions of space is that objects are organized and utilized according to a logic that is similar to the dynamic of history itself, in which the continuity of space is guaranteed. Thus, objects form space and, conversely, space forms the objects. Systems of objects condition actions in a constant dialogue, enabling the transformation of existing objects and leading to the creation of new ones. Lefebvre and Santos's definition of space is part of a body of work which underpins the idea that space and society are mutually formed and transformed. As Rob Shields (2013: 41) puts it, 'changes in experience and philosophy have altered spatial perception and thought, changing social behavior, architecture, planning and settlement patterns several times since Pythagoras'.

Space is formed by and mediates our relations with other beings, entities and flows. Walking through vast expanses of desert, or during a long night of dreams, we are aware of our existence through the entities a nd flows that make up space. When we imagine, or dream, without conscious control over our acts and mental activities, we seem detached from the material space. Quite often we base our imagination on the known world, formed by entities and flows we experience while awake, which serve as references of our mental activity. Nonetheless, there are oneiric elements that belong only to the dream world, but which inform our conscious life. Robert Walser – whose writing about art in the early-twentieth century is not that of a critic explaining or dissecting or discussing a painting, but instead a narration from within, and from his idiosyncratic point of view – looks at his brother's painting, *The Dream* (from 1903), which depicts a boy and a woman crossing a vaulted bridge in the evening, and writes: 'I was like a dream within a dream, like one thought embedded in another. (. . .) I was like a scent, a feeling; I was like the feeling in the heart of the lady who was thinking of me' (Walser, 2015).

The idea that space can include human experiences such as dreams and religious beliefs, together with forests and physics and mathematical theories is a challenging one. But we do inhabit, form and are formed by multiple spaces. Let us start with the scientific mathematical space, which has precise rules – albeit transformed over the centuries – and whose formation contains two essential points: it defines what the describable objects and actions are, which therefore form part of the space (with no room for dreams), while at the same time conveying the idea of infinite space.

Leaving out the human feelings and beliefs about how we perceive and experience space diminishes the validity of any general concept of space. And it also makes the notion of infinite space more challenging: if space is infinite, there can be nothing outside it and nothing beyond it. If there is nothing outside space, if it is infinite, are dreams part of the space? Or would it be infinite only within the realms of a particular notion of space – such as the physical or astronomical? But if there is a 'within', it is not infinite. The conundrum of tying together a theoretical infinite space and an experienced space seems to echo the opinion of the philosopher Jan Marejko (1994), for whom infinite space is a prison that takes on the force of despair, since all the questions about it would be part of that space, would be subordinate to it and would lead nowhere.

Edward Hall's works (1959; 1966) are appropriate here. Space is one of the dimensions of human interaction with the surrounding environment and with other humans. But Hall makes it clear that space is not the same for all humankind, but actually varies according to culture, to an extent that it might influence linguistic structures – and, consequently, linguistic differences may influence non-linguistic spatial cognition. Karen Emmorey (2004) gives the example of the Mayan language Tzeltal, which lacks concepts such as left, right, front and back, using absolute coordinates instead. Even for small-location descriptors, such as the position of a spoon in relation to a plate, Tzeltal speakers use 'the spoon is north of the plate'. Another example comes from the Inuit, who speak one of the four remaining native languages spoken in Canada. Living in snowy expanses that look homogeneous to most people, the Inuit have such careful visual attention that spatial characteristics are embedded in their language, with 'location and orientation of an object as part of the grammatical structure of a sentence' (Ellard, 2009: 39). They also learn to recognize patterns in open water and wind, in the refraction and reflection on snowy terrains. The Micmac, another indigenous people living in Canada, name trees according to the sound of the wind when it blows through their branches in the fall, 'an hour after the sunset during those weeks when the weather comes always from a certain direction'

16   Constructions

(Davis, 2001: 10). And as trees grow and decay, or the weather changes through the years, the names of the trees also change.

The human experience is central to the work of Yi-Fu Tuan (1977). His books are important for anyone dedicated to the study of space, but his constant mixing together of different concepts (such as space and place) means that they should be read with care. For someone so attuned to the human experience above any purely intellectual endeavour in defining space, his thoughts on a daily experience such as the time spent sleeping might be helpful, not only for questioning his reasoning, but for opening up other possible understandings of the multiple spaces we live in. Tuan (1983) accepts that when a man (*sic*) is sleeping he is still influenced by the surroundings, but loses his world and is reduced to the status of a body occupying a space. Now, more than half a century after the writings of Freud, this statement should immediately be questioned; for sleep, which Lefebvre (1981: 24) indicates as one of philosophy's puzzles, since it 'reproduces pre-natal life and presages death', is an everyday experience that can serve as an example of the different systems of objects and actions, of different entities and flows that humans experience, and with which we construct our spaces.

The sleeping body occupies space not, by simply being outstretched and inert, but because at that moment, even while being an unconscious mind, the body maintains active exchanges with its surroundings. The body actively establishes relations with space in order to remain in equilibrium and continue working. The body regulates its temperature, which is different from that when we are performing conscious activities, changes breathing rhythms and chooses sleep positions (seated or lying, not standing) in spite of the mind being unconscious. Indeed, even while sleeping we are still alert to the world we know when awake, albeit minimally. We still relate our surroundings to our biological filters, for we are immediately wakened by strange external noises or physiological requirements. So, even with a body considered inert by Tuan, we are not merely 'occupying a space' but are dealing with entities and flows in the best possible way to retain wellbeing – and certainly a large number of elements with which we are not concerned when awake.

Sleep also involves other aspects of what space is, of what forms space. The research of Peter Kraftl and John Horton (2008) on the geography of sleep encompasses studies ranging from sleep as a post-medical therapeutic process and everyday small routines, to the architecture of sleep, focusing on the design of spaces dedicated to sleeping (from bedrooms to airports), and how people appropriate these spaces. Moreover, with sleep come dreams, which have a well-established importance in understanding human psychology. We dream when arriving at a particular level of disconnection from the world experienced consciously – indeed, during *rapid eye movement* (REM) sleep our brain is more active than in previous non-REM sleeping phases. Moreover, deprivation of REM sleep impairs long-term memory and complex thinking.

In one of his short stories, Edgar Alan Poe (1850: 311–12) wrote that

> He who has never swooned, is not he who finds strange palaces and wildly familiar faces in coals that glow; [. . .] is not he who ponders over the perfume of some novel flower – is not he whose brain grows bewildered with the meaning of some musical cadence which has never before arrested his attention.

The world of dreams has long been important in the cultural formation of peoples and individuals. Based on her work with the Mapuche in Chile, Irène Hirt (2012) discusses the incorporation of dreams and dreaming practices as sources of geographical information. Her work is part of a broad attempt to incorporate indigenous mapping techniques into mainstream scientific cartography. Dreams as sources of territorial knowledge can be found among indigenous peoples from Alaska to Australia. In the case of the Mapuche, Hirt found internalized prejudices against their own cultural practices. *Pewma* is the Mapuche word for dreams with special individual or collective significance, through which knowledge is transmitted to wise persons – such as the chiefs and shamans. And 'because Mapuche dreamers are said to be connected with beings inhabiting other places or spheres of the universe, they have privileged access to geographical information' (Hirt, 2012: 112), and dreamlike dimensions have been incorporated into the mapping process of Mapuche land.

In his novel *Dictionary of the Khazars*, Milorad Pavić (1988) tells of the controversy involving the nomadic Khazar warrior people, who 'imagine the future in terms of space, never time' (145). In the eighth or ninth century CE, the chief of the Khazars had an enigmatic dream that seemed to relate to the fate of his people. He called three philosophers, a Christian, a Jew and a Muslim, and decided that the Khazars would convert to the religion of the one who deciphered the dream. They were dream hunters who 'could read other people's dreams, live and make themselves at home in them, and through the dreams hunt the game that was their prey – a human, an object, or an animal'. The most famous hunter, Al Safer, who tamed fish in people's dreams, found God in the deep spaces of dreams and became lost there, not through any mistake during his ascension to God, but through not knowing how to return.

18   Constructions

Shamans, decipherers and dream hunters try to discover the mysteries of a world that seems so human but is still mostly enclosed in the oneiric realm. Shamans in the Bavarian Alps in the fifteenth and sixteenth centuries did not conceal their associations with nocturnal entities, 'so sure were they of the legitimacy of their magical night companions and journeys' (Koslofsky, 2011: 30). With the dominance of the Church, the rules of the modern state and scientific knowledge across Europe, mutual interferences of the secular and magical worlds became connected either to witchcraft or to less-developed peoples. Although dreams acquired scientific importance again in the twentieth century with the psychoanalysis of Sigmund Freud, their incorporation as a source of knowledge (as in the case of the Mapuche) is rare. The incorporation of dreams, and the unconscious impulses and stimuli that give them life, either into or as other spatial systems we live in, presents an intellectual challenge rather than prejudice against traditional forms of knowledge. But dreams can intervene in the behaviour of the body and its interaction with the surroundings, inducing movement, temperature changes, and perspiration that are experienced between the different spaces which are lived in simultaneously. It is also undeniable that the experience of dreams affects how we deal with space when awake.

Even Henri Lefebvre acknowledged the importance of the world of dreams, which is both fictional and real at the same time. However, concerned with the social practices that constitute space, he does not consider it important for 'social learning' (Lefebvre, 1981: 240), and therefore not a constituent of space. Taking into account the previous examples of indigenous peoples, our cultural struggle to incorporate dreams as an element of space is particularly true in the modern society considered by Lefebvre. Without that proviso his points dismissing dreams as constituents of space seem to have universal validity – which is not the case.

Dreams are out of the scope of this book simply because the cultural system addressed here (modern, western and urban) does not consider them as a collective factor. It does not imply that oneiric entities and flows do not constitute space; it simply means that I set them aside when framing my field of inquiry. Thus, it should be emphasized that the inclusion or exclusion of one or more elements in the constitution of space does not occur because of their atavistic values or because of the existence of a universal logic of space. When we frame the field of inquiry we select the collective cultural filters of the world under consideration, which include or exclude certain elements. This is, therefore, a methodological and theoretical decision, not an inalienable logical principle of space.

Space is perceived through biological filters, as well as through cultural filters, which differ from species to species, from culture to culture. Some

Constructions 19

animals use magnetic fields, or differences in certain sound or light waves to perceive and experience space – characteristics that are not screened through human biological filters. On the other hand, some of our less-evident senses, such as the vestibular system, are crucial to our spatial experience – even though not considered in the common discussion about human senses. As the astronaut Jeffrey Hoffman (2004) noted, the vestibular system, which maintains our balance on Earth, immediately suffers in conditions of lack of gravity, causing nausea and disorientation. Biological filters are context-based, as we have seen with the Inuit aptitude for deciphering visual details in a landscape most of us see as homogeneous.

We could be said to live in potentially different spaces according to biological and cultural filters. Returning briefly to the example of sleep, we could be said to live in three different spaces while sleeping (even though, as a person, they are interconnected): the space of the sleeping body, which interacts physically with the surroundings; the dream space, populated by internalized entities, and flows/actions that often influence the space we live in when conscious. These three spaces feedback into each other, even though they are normally seen and analyzed separately.

Perhaps because they are experienced in everyday terms, in a single body, this distinction between spaces might be helpful as a methodological device. Let us consider an astronomer. When the Sun rises he awakens, he cycles off to his laboratory, having to avoid cars, controlling the power of his legs to go uphill and downhill, taking natural or architectural elements as references, experiencing a space composed of corporeal and urban flows and entities. He powers up the computers, looks at the sky through a telescope and immerses himself in a world of solar explosions, the transformation of hydrogen into helium, the effect of solar plasma on the Earth's gravitational field, the courses of natural and artificial satellites, studying how these elements relate to each other and organize astronomical space. Although conceivable, it seems disproportionate to think how and why the thermal balance of the sleeping human body could be included as an element that has any influence on the astronomical space studied by the astronomer. The apprehension, comprehension and analysis of spaces accept that the astronomer experiences different spaces – different because they are formed of entities and flows organized according to specific logics, which are determined by cultural filters, and with different purposes. And even knowing about the rotation of the Earth, at the end of the working day the astronomer cycles off into the sunset.

We can now attempt a definition of space that encompasses all living beings: space is formed by the enactment, the dynamic articulations of entities (natural and man-made, material and immaterial) and flows

20 *Constructions*

(spontaneous and intentional) strained through the biological and cultural filters of living beings. Analyzing each term of this definition, we might say:

- Entities are elements of reference, individual or collective singularities, that may be natural or man-made, material or immaterial, whose characteristics are perceived by living beings (human or nonhumans), directly or through other entities (such as technological artefacts). Examples range from stars and bicycles to mythical characters.
- Flows are any kind of exchange that circulates among entities. Flows might serve as markers and catalysts; for instance, temperature variation [flow] in a room is felt because it interacts with a warm-blooded body [entity] that recognizes this variation and searches for temperature balance. The interaction of entities and flows is what enacts space, and is simultaneously promoted by space itself.
- We apprehend some and not other entities and flows due to our sensorial and cultural filters, which differ between species, people and human groups.

Edward Hall argues that sensorial filters vary according to cultural contexts and backgrounds, and that consequently people from different cultures use senses differently. According to Hall (1966), Japanese have an acoustic spatial perception for which simple paper walls provide insulation, while in northern Europe this insulation requires a thick wall; or the olfactory space valued by Arabs enables a 'chemical sense' that has been minimized in western culture. Kevin Lynch's findings on how people build images of the cities they live in were based mainly on visual elements. The prevalence of the sense of sight is not inherent to how humans perceive space, but to the culture Lynch's subjects live in, which influenced both Lynch's methods and the subjects' responses: modern, western and urban life. In Japan, authors (Kido, 2012; Ueda, 2014) still consider that the appreciation of natural phenomena such as rainfall, snowfall and seasonal colours influences how people perceive space, incorporating a temporal factor in how people apprehend and appreciate the landscape – a perceptual experience the authors argue that has been changing in major urban centres with the reconstruction following World War II, which mainly followed modern and westernized urban principles.

The perception of elements other than those normally accepted within a particular culture led the geographer André Siegfried (1947) to suggest that geography concerns itself with any objects/entities and actions/flows organized in space; therefore, why not a geography of sounds, colours or smells? A spatial distribution of scents would vary in space and time, with the characteristic smell of the French Second Empire still found in the old cafés of the early-twentieth century, and which Siegfried found in Mexico as an indication of the French presence there. Sissel Tolaas has been archiving smells for over 25 years, and has now catalogued thousands of distinctive smells from all over the world, with the purpose of creating a 'smell language'. This catalogue allows Tolaas to create olfactory maps – against what she calls 'bland scapes', areas void of stimuli, characterized by an anguished sense of placelessness. In 2001 Tolaas mapped the smells of Mexico City, based on constant visits to its neighbourhoods, collecting chemical signals of the environment, and interviewing people describing what they smell.

A wide range of spatial perceptions is still present outside mainstream modern urban culture, such as the water diviners in rural Africa, who can pinpoint the location of groundwater sources by pointing a forked stick to the ground. And it is still quite common in rural Brazil to find people who can tell by the breeze or birdsong whether it is going to rain. All these examples show that the same space is apprehended in different ways through sensorial and cultural filters. Flows and entities (natural and man-made, material and immaterial) are potentially present for everyone in any of those situations; but some people or groups are able to apprehend particular elements and include them in their spatial system, whereas in other groups the same elements pass unnoticed.

Returning to the constitution of space, there is firstly a plethora of elements, which can be divided into entities and flows. People's sensorial filters apprehend some of these elements, while missing others – an unconscious selection that might vary according to the context people live in, and to their cultural background. Flows and entities apprehended by people are organized according to the relationships they establish with each other. Space is the enactment of flows and entities; and people, or other living beings that apprehend such elements, intervene in this enactment, playing a crucial role in the construction of spatial systems.

People live in different spatial systems depending on immediate purposes, as in the case of the astronomer riding his bicycle to the astronomy laboratory, living in both urban and astronomical spaces which barely relate to each other. Furthermore, the spatial perceptions of people from the same cultural base in a common space also differ, according to the keenness with which they use their senses. Edward Hall mentions a blind man who manages to apprehend a space but whose identification of the flows and material entities is restricted to a few metres, perceived through smell, sound or touch (both physical and through the vibrations felt by the body). Within the same space, a sighted person would potentially consider a greater number of elements, although

22   Constructions

setting aside stimuli that are fundamental to the constitution of space to the blind. Of course, the use of more senses enables a broader apprehension of space, but the skill of specific senses can bring a qualitative richness to a sensory experience of space, which differs depending on the senses one privileges or is able to use. Patrick Süskind's novel *Perfume* (1986) comes to mind. It tells the story of a gifted boy who could decipher eighteenth-century Paris through its plethora of smells, which led to his becoming a perfumer, but also drove him to the obsession of capturing the scent of a young lady.

The spatial differences provided by the use of the senses can also be illustrated by Edgar Allen Poe's *The Pit and the Pendulum* (1850) and by Werner Herzog's film *The Enigma of Kaspar Hauser* (1974). In both cases, we can see how our sensorial filters are closely tied to our cultural background. In Poe's story, a prisoner on trial loses his senses. His last image is of the seven candles on the judge's table; his consciousness slowly evades, and 'then silence, and stillness, night were the universe'. Taken asleep to a dark room, on wakening he first perceives sound, motion and touch and only then he is conscious of his existence, 'without thought'. He is afraid to open his eyes, not for fear of what he might see, but for fear that there should be nothing to see. Opening his eyes to the complete darkness, he begins to discover where he is through touch, making out the different shapes of stones forming an uneven wall, leading him to believe he is in a large room, without ever finding the centre. He falls senseless. On regaining consciousness a faint gleam of light enters the room and reveals it to be much smaller than he had perceived through touch. The tactile irregularity of the stones had led him to believe he was in a much larger space. And at the centre of the room he had not reached before, he now sees a deep pit.

The Enigma of Kaspar Hauser is based on the story of a boy who appeared in Nuremberg, Germany, in 1828, claiming to have lived locked in a tiny, damp, dark, dirty cell. Herzog's film begins with Hauser's removal from the cell and his discovery of the other elements that comprise the outside space, which had not been part of his own. The key scene here is when Hauser looks at the outside of the tower and says that it is much smaller on the outside than on the inside, for now he can manage to see it in its entirety, while when he lived inside it, in his cell, the tower surrounded him and he never saw it at one glance.

In both cases, spatial perception changes according to the elements each character can filter. Also in both cases, the apprehension of space occurs firstly through pure senses – coincidently, in both, through touch. This material apprehension of the world relates to Edward Hall's (1959) difficulty in understanding why the Greeks had no pictorial work of the same importance as their sculptures. The ways humans apprehend the world correspond therefore to how the world is represented. Apprehension is immediate, and representation is mediate; however, once a form of representation becomes prevalent, it shapes the way we understand the world and shape our culture. Privileging visual expressions of the surrounding world has arguably made sight dominate other senses in perceiving the world in the modern western context.

A contemporary of Edward Hall, Marshall McLuhan (1964) wrote that technologies are primarily extensions of our senses. We apprehend space through our biological senses and their technological extensions. It is true that technologies put something between our body and the world. But Hall's works made it clear that our sensory relations with the surroundings have cultural components. The astronaut Jeffrey Hoffman, although valuing the presence of humans in outer space, highlights the importance of technological devices in obtaining first-hand data from the universe. Technologies do not remove our innermost contact with the material world if we agree with Hoffman (2004: 150) on the importance of understanding 'how our unique biochemical-based minds can interact with machines to project our consciousness to realms we cannot physically reach'.

On the one hand the prevalence of sight might make us unaware of the olfactory or tactile qualities of space; on the other hand, simple devices such as telescopes enhance vision beyond any human capacity. The history of humankind is marked by the changes in tools we use for apprehending, understanding and controlling the world. Our history can be told through the history of technologies, the extensions of human senses proposed by McLuhan. Technologies first and foremost reveal dimensions and qualities of the world inaccessible to the human mind and body, eventually changing how we perceive and conceive the world around us.

The telescope is an extension of human sight that reveals astronomical entities and flows inaccessible to the naked eye, transforming not only what we can apprehend and know about outer space, but also transforming our understanding of ourselves. Gustave Flaubert said that the more the telescope developed the more stars appeared. It would be easy to say that all the stars were already there before they could be seen – but perceiving them, experiencing them through extensions of human senses, make them effectively constituents of the world – and how we understand it. Yi-Fu Tuan (1977) stresses the importance of experiencing space by suggesting the challenge of breaking with a degree of analytical thought for which 'knowing' means 'knowing about'. Knowing presupposes exploring the unknown, whilst knowing about presupposes a previous conceptual framework, in which case many stimuli are lost because they cannot fit into the concepts of the physical sciences.

24 Constructions

Technological extensions of our senses, like the telescope, have been developed largely through mathematical hypotheses of the existence of elements that have not yet been experienced, but which must exist. Conceiving such elements prior to experiencing their existence directly through human senses implies that humans use another technological instrument, the most important we possess: language. Language mediates our relations with other entities, and through language we can envision entities and phenomena we have not yet experienced. It is through language that various constituent elements of the world, of space, pass through a filter constructed largely by language itself, and are considered to be real, and they can only be experienced through technological instruments. Likewise, technologies do not separate humans from the world, but instead bring humans to yet unknown characteristics of the world.

Technological devices that extend our senses allow the inclusion of entities and flows previously alien to our spatial system. The Milky Way is composed of gas, cosmic dust and around 400 billion suns responsible for the gravitational energy of a much greater number of asteroids, satellites and planets – one of which is Earth, where the human being is one of the fifty billion species that inhabit it (Sagan, 1997). Humans are the only species able to conceive that universe and describe part of its organization with the aid of instruments launched into space for exploring these astrophysical worlds; and quite often these technologies discover elements still unimaginable in astronomical space. These instruments are what allow theories to be tested, sometimes extending the human senses – like spaceships to Mars or men landing on the Moon. These technologies explore space through representation – a mediated exploration of space.

In a more mundane example, automobiles extended the spatial range, and decreased the time consumed to cover distances, with lesser burdens on city dwellers than animal- and steam-powered vehicles, to an extent that this technology reshaped our understanding of urban space. Cities were redesigned, destroyed and rebuilt to accommodate motorized traffic. The automobile, and the speed that comes with it, altered how we apprehend space, adjusting which entities and flows we filter while travelling. In a simple experience of walking along a road or travelling on it at 100 kilometres per hour, various objects are apprehended that are mutually exclusive: and those that are common are dealt with differently, even though the origin, destination and path of the journey are the same.

The basic theoretical foundation of this book is that space is constructed through the relationships between entities and flows, that these elements are apprehended in different ways according to sensorial and cultural filters, and that the enactment of these entities and flows depends on purposes and specific logics – urban spaces and astronomical spaces are defined by distinctive entities and flows. Regardless of purposes or specific logics, space can be conceived of synthetically, serving therefore as a conceptual and methodological tool for understanding multiple spatial phenomena. This synthetic definition is polyvalent from the outset. Spatial systems differ according to the sensory characteristics of different species and individuals, according to the cultural characteristics of groups, and within the same group, or for individuals, according to the purposes and to which logics are used for the apprehension and comprehension of entities and flows – again, the astronomer perceives different entities and flows when considering the world within different logics.

We have shown the importance of first-hand apprehension of entities and flows through our senses in the construction of space. Nonetheless, it is equally valid to explore space through language, through intellectual enquiry, and in its most abstract forms.

A brief return to astronomy, even without deep scientific knowledge, can shed some light on this. John Brockman (1986) begins his book with the necessary demystification of science as the conveyor of absolute truths, stating that each era creates its own universe. In ancient Greece, Eudoxus imagined a firmament of twenty-seven invisible spheres organized around the Earth. Copernicus rejected this theory in the late-fifteenth century, destroying the spheres and placing the Sun at the centre of the universe. Two centuries later, Newton showed that the movement of the celestial bodies, as well as any object on Earth, is governed by principles that could be described mathematically. In the twentieth century Einstein demonstrated that space is not a 'nothing' in which the Earth moves, but that it has laws that influence the actual existence and dynamics of Earth; and in 1979 Alan Guth suggested that moments before the creation of the universe, some 10^{-35} of a second, there was an inflation of the universe in expansion, giving mathematical proof to the Big Bang theory (Brockman, 1986). While accepting the Big Bang, Carl Sagan (1997) recalls that scientists think that this is perhaps valid for a particular universe, which might be one among an infinite number; while some are in permanent expansion, others grow to a point of collapse and others are perhaps already in a state of balance, with cyclical expansions and contractions – such as our own, counting its 15 billion years from its present 'incarnation', after that Big Bang.

From Copernicus to Einstein, the universe and space were apprehended according to ideas held about them, according to the mathematical representations that could be made of them and according to the cultural values embedded in their respective societies, which pervaded even their scientific thinking. Rob Shields (2013: 56) argues that Newton's description of a pure, homogeneous and absolute space, containing anything without changing itself, reflects that the 'attributes of God brought a level of cosmological completeness and perfection'. And despite the relevance of Leibniz's critiques of Newton's ideas of a pure and absolute space, preferring to define space as a network of relations among things, Shields shows that as Newton's ideas were useful to astronomy and everyday physics, such criticisms were largely ignored for a long time.

We might be living through a similar moment: theories, experiments, and representations of relativity and quantum physics seem so separate from our daily and sensory experience that it is difficult to incorporate them into the common conception and, moreover, into the apprehension and understanding of space. Moving from cross-disciplinary theories to practice is once again a major challenge in spatial studies (Shields, 2013).

As we have mentioned, an essential point in the construction of space concerns how it is represented through language. Language can be described as the replacement of an object by one or multiple signs that enable it to be investigated, understood and have some of its features transmitted to other people. Through language, the features of objects and phenomena can be shared and promote better understanding of them, even without their presence. John Casti (1997) stresses that scientific representation tends towards models that remove some features of the real world, but through which reality can be experienced, explained and envisaged. The aim of representation is to achieve those three levels. The Darwinian model of evolution and natural selection explains the survival of some species and the extinction of others, although it is unable to predict species' behaviour by changing such conditions. Newton's model of the movement of the planets allows navigators and astronomers to predict where they will be by knowing the position of the Sun at a given moment. The understanding of astronomical space from Eudoxus to Einstein shows that scientific breakthroughs are often accompanied by profound changes in scientific representation. Fostered by emerging concepts, representation to a large extent preceded experience of space, of possible spaces. This is the case of black holes, 'gravitationally contracting stars', so dense that they suck in any element passing close to them, including light. They were described in 1915 by Karl Schwarzchild on his deathbed, imagining a body with such powerful gravitational force that it would contract – 'even beyond the web of space itself' (Brockman, 1986: 48). The world of astrophysics subsequently sought to prove their existence, which only occurred in 1973. As an essential element in understanding astronomical space, their representation precedes experience of them. Representation enables the construction of spaces not directly perceived by the senses.

Eudoxus and Guth spoke of the same flows and entities, and both had the same western cultural basis, although centuries apart; but how they accepted them, how they apprehended them, how they fitted them into astronomical space in such different ways leads one to ask whether Eudoxus and Guth are talking about the same space. If one were to consider the elements accepted by each of them, the way they organized them, to form a space different from other spaces experienced by humans, the answer is no; if one considers that this accepted distinction still determines that astronomical space can largely be understood without considering other elements belonging to the cities, the answer is yes: two logics affecting what is considered as part of space.

As we have been discussing, different spatial systems coexist simultaneously, with no hierarchical difference. It is really difficult, if not impossible, to accommodate contemporary theories of physics about space with oneiric elements still important for some people in mapping their territories. Considerable intellectual openness is required to admit that both are part of the human endeavour to define a primal component of our existence: space. The astronomer who bicycles to the laboratory selects different entities and flows that make up urban spaces and astrophysical ones, which cannot be combined – even though he, the astronomer, experiences both of them. The construction of space is therefore disconnected from the domination of particular social systems – which ultimately characterizes the production of Lefebvre's space. As Stuart Elden (2004: 181) notes on Lefebvre's theory, 'the production of space is a theme that has explicit political aspects, and is related to developing a system of production within capitalism'; and that for Lefebvre space is 'the ultimate locus and medium of struggle, and is therefore a political issue' (183).

Christian Schimd (2008) pointed out that Lefebvre's dialectic of space treats how space is perceived, conceived and lived equally. Lefebvre's works re-establish that space is a product, since it contains a mode of domination of one cultural group over another, with all the values being accepted as inherent to its constituent elements. Lefebvre's argument that space is a social construction sometimes seems to be bounded by a particular society he is concerned with – or, as Lukasz Stanek (2011: 81) puts it, his 'wording' belongs to a 'highly cultural and historical context'. The challenge remains the same as that cherished by Lefebvre himself: the need for universal concepts as epistemological tools for understanding the world; epistemological tools that will inevitably be circumscribed by historical context, but which should not be taken as inevitable truth.

The paradox of space is that it is both the most abstract and the most tangible of the three main spatial concepts discussed in this book: space, place and territory. Space is the epistemological matrix upon which other

28   *Constructions*

related concepts (such as place and territory) are constructed, whereas it is also apprehended instinctively and immediately by our senses – and their technological extensions – which is not the case with place and territory, as we will see.

We feel space before thinking of it. Our relation with space is visceral. Space is constructed through the relationship between entities and flows, which are apprehended through sensorial and cultural filters. Indeed, as in any human relation with the world, we attribute signs to the elements that pass through these filters – when we touch a rough surface we attribute the quality of roughness in comparison with a repertoire of textures we have previously experienced. But the process of apprehending spatial qualities precedes the process of signification that seeks to attribute meanings to entities and flows (as we will discuss later, this is the defining process of places and territories).

Therefore, we can now say that the construction of space has three basic points: its perception by the senses and their extensions; its comprehension as an exclusive qualitative system (preceding the attribution of meanings to the relationships established between entities and flows); and its representation through language, which allows it to be described and envisioned, even when it cannot be experienced directly by the senses.

Along this chapter, certain spaces, such as those of dreams and astronomy, were singled out to support the validity of the synthetic concept of space, with entities and flows strained through sensorial and cultural filters, and depending on particular logics – an astronomer uses different sensorial and cultural filters when he is cycling to the laboratory and when he is exploring outer space. Thus, although it is the most immediate of the spatial concepts, our apprehension of space has a degree of mediation: sensorial and cultural filters. Equipped with the appropriate conceptual instruments it is possible to work on the filter itself to determine which elements will be considered. This is what the astronomer in our example does: he uses specific filters that select some entities and flows while discarding all the others. Expressing a well-known dilemma among architects, urban planners and other practitioners involved in designing space, Bernard Tschumi (1994: 28) points to a more general paradox of 'questioning the nature of space and at the same time experiencing a spatial praxis'. In this case, the architect is selecting entities and flows which will be apprehended by the user while discarding all the others; he is privileging particular sensorial and cultural filters. Bad architecture simply tries to paste meanings onto space, whereas good architecture changes how we filter entities and flows, designing the way we apprehend and comprehend a fundamental feature of our world: space.

Having defined space, we might now move to the other two spatial concepts discussed in this book: place and territory.

The construction of place

Place, in tandem with space and territory, is one of the fundamental spatial concepts through which we define ourselves. I begin this chapter with a straightforward definition of place, which will be carefully refined throughout the text.

Place is a portion of space to which a person or a group of people attribute particular values through which they identify themselves, and identify this portion of space as constituent of their shared values. Place is a primal feature of human beings – and even other living beings. Being in a place is both informative and formative. Informative because the cultural values attributed to a portion of space invest it with additional layers of information that are not intrinsic to it (different people and groups might attribute different values to the same portion of space, as we will discuss later); and formative because once these layers are shared by different people, they reiterate such values within the group.

This definition of place is a more complex way of defining it than simply as a geographical position of a body in relation to other bodies, objects, and the whole space (as usually heard in daily conversations). Such a reductionist approach can be alleviated, though, if we consider place as a form of subjective positioning of oneself into the world, and an engagement with the world.

Joseph Rykwert (1976: 54) explains that in Mesopotamia, founders of towns 'consulted the flight of birds, the movement of stray animals, thunder perhaps, the motion of the clouds, to find out if the site and day were propitious' to their endeavour. And on top of that, there was liver divination – all parts of the rituals of founding a town, as a way of impregnating a portion of space with cultural values. Keith Lilley (2014) states that among Jews and Christians cities were full of the hierarchical symbolism between the macrocosm of the universe, the cosmic body and the microcosm of the human body. The shape of Jerusalem was seen as symmetrical to the shape of the world. In that way, place is less defined by its form, but by the values that shape any resulting form. Place is a medium through which we as a person or a group position ourselves within geographical, cultural, emotional universes.

John Agnew (1987; 2012) both dissociates and respects the relationship between the cultural and geographical aspects embedded in the notion of place by proposing three terms that encompass the complex relation of being in a place. Location as the position one occupies in space, 'where an activity or object is located and which relates to other sites or

30   *Constructions*

locations' (Agnew, 2012: 89), locale as the setting where social relations happen, 'where everyday life takes place' (2012: 89), and sense of place as the emotional relationship people have with specific portions of space, of 'identification with a place as a unique community, landscape and moral order' (2012: 89).

Projecting values onto a portion of space leads to place being frequently considered as a safe location, while space is interpreted as boundless and therefore open to the unknown. For Edward Casey (1993: 3), the security of place contrasts with the indistinct 'soup of space', where all references are lost; and he adds that 'Just as there can be no experience in time except as the time of events in places, so there can be no sense of space that is not anchored, finally if not immediately, in particular places' (288). Tim Cresswell (2004: 12) defines place as 'how we make the world meaningful and the way we experience the world.'

Despite his insightful works, Casey often opposes places to space instead of seeing the two as complementary concepts. In this regards, it seems Casey uses place more as a synonym to location – a place located somewhere. On the other hand, Cresswell argues that the attribution of meaning to places has to be seen in a 'context of power'. As I discuss later, power is more related to the concept of territory, though. Treating place and space as coexisting and complementary concepts, not contradictory, makes them epistemological tools to understand the world. Therefore, it is useful to differentiate, but not oppose, place from space to make both concepts clear.

Perception plays a key role in differentiating space and places. Lucrécia Ferrara (1993: 107–108) writes that space is marked by the percept, while place is marked by perceptive judgment. The former appears through its 'poly-sensory impact', while the latter is already based on the awareness of the action of perception in which 'the quality of the object becomes the element that distinguishes it from others of the same kind, and through which it acquires value'. Ferrara (1993: 153) stresses 'it is necessary to go beyond that overall evenness of space to discover the places in which information materializes.' These remarks bring us to the underlying idea of this book that space, territory and place do not exist as autonomous entities, but are mutually formative, and each of them is constructed and becomes part of our existence in the world through biological, subjective or intellectual engagement with entities and flows, objects and actions.

In this sense, the understanding of the construction of place as an intellectual operation can be used as a conceptual tool in studying how people or groups define and are defined by spatial features. Space, experienced by the percept, contains qualitative stimuli bearing no definitive meaning. At first, all stimuli are equivalent. After this initial moment when all perceptual stimuli are worth the same, the sensory and intellectual representation of space, through images, sounds or smells, leads to a selection of particular entities and flows, which are organized in particular ways, according to a set of values. This process triggers the attribution of meaning to particular spatial features; and this, in turn, leads to the initial phase of the establishment of places, when these features acquire different meanings for different people, based on their experiences.

Walter Benjamin's montage of the image of the city describes and gives meaning to the galleries, streets and monuments of the metropolis. This enables a reading and understanding of the urban space through some of its parts, chosen and described as a way of reflecting the user, who experiences cities through their subjective fragmentation, through their places.

Kevin Lynch (1960) studied how residents of three North American cities selected and organized particular physical elements, how they fragmented the urban space according to their perception and values. Lynch based his study on people's representations of the same portions of space, usually their sketches, which highlighted specific spatial features. Lynch identified the common spatial references and ways of reading space presented in these sketches, and grouped them as paths, edges, districts, nodes and landmarks. Lynch's works revealed how subjectivity influences what it is that makes space unique to different people, mixing formalist and subjective avenues for exploring the urban environment.

Twenty-five years after the publication of his seminal work, Lynch (1990) addressed the main critiques his book received, and accepts mainly two: one is that his research method and findings were inadvertently used as an enclosed design technique, rather than opening a new channel of communication between citizens and planners; and another was that his method did not take into account that the perception of the city changes over time, and it therefore does not explain how a certain pattern was achieved or what might happen in a near future due to ongoing social transformations, for instance.

Nevertheless, the main critique of Lynch's method is his conviction that a 'distinctive and legible environment not only offers security but also heightens the potential depth and intensity of human experience' (Lynch, 1960: 5). The Brazilian anthropologist Roberto DaMatta (1991) showed how people navigate within slums, a human settlement far from legible according to Lynch's principles, using other signifiers, from sounds to key-people's houses and social behaviour. And one cannot say their experience of space is less profound or less intense than the spatial experience of people living in distinctive and legible environments. Spatial distinctiveness and legibility depend on users' cultural

32   Constructions

backgrounds, which will determine the elements they take into account when experiencing space.

But the use of physical components of the city as independent variables for explaining urban vivacity, and even the urban character, continued to expand in the following years. Also in the United States, William Whyte (1984) used a 16 mm camera and a more standardized protocol to understand which physical elements, and how they are organized, make certain parts of the city more utilized and cherished by so many people. Whyte focused on plazas and small parks. He counted benches and their position and width, mapped areas of sun and shade, and noted the presence and placement of water surfaces, achieving a catalogue of good practices that would make certain portions of space more likely to be used than others. The underlying idea is how to make memorable places out of anonymous spaces. Others have used similar methods to assess and prescribe urban qualities which would make people more likely to use certain areas of the city (Gehl, 2010).

Although Whyte's focus on the material qualities that make a portion of space more used than others is an important contribution to urban design, besides a few peculiar characters present in public spaces Whyte monitored (the guardian, the fool, the lonely talking man, the street vendor), this genre of work tends to leave aside broader social characteristics of the region where these plazas and parks are located. Indeed, Whyte acknowledges that scale might be a challenge to the existence of vibrant public spaces in small towns: 'Where 3,000 people an hour pass by a site, a lot of mistakes can be made in design and a place may still end up being well used' (Whyte, 1980: 90). But even in the same city, plazas with identical physical components are used differently (or not at all), depending on the social, cultural and religious characteristics of those living in the area. Even within a population with the same cultural background, usage changes depending on the land use of the surrounding area – a residential neighbourhood and the central business district have dissimilar uses, which also vary in intensity during the week and hours of the day. More than the presence and organization of objects, it is the attribution of cultural signs to a portion of space that makes people construct places within the vast space.

Understanding that a single portion of space might contain multiple collections of complementary, contradictory and overlapping places is in a way a critique of the typical urban plans of modernism. Modernist urban plans organized space in definitive, hierarchical forms, with little if any consideration of the way space would in fact be apprehended, used and transformed by its occupants, which would vary according to their cultural backgrounds and aspirations.

Building on Heidegger, Elden (2001: 85) explains space as place freed for settlement and lodging. Jan Marejko (1994: 32) emphasizes the importance of place in relation to an abstract space referring to modern space as a quest for utopia (being in all places) through the construction of atopy (being in no place). And Henri Lefebvre (1981: 261 onwards) sees the formal freedom of the modern architectural space as the homogeneous model of capitalist space, ready to engineer every person in its 'machines for living' into a totalitarian space devoid of places. In Jacques Tati's film *Mon Oncle* (1958), Monsieur Hulot visits his sister Madame Arpel's new house. It fits perfectly into the modernist model of a 'machine for living', full of equipments that control not only how the building functions, but how the dwellers behave as well. As Denis Martouzet and Georges-Henry Laffont (2010) put it, the Arpel's house and their modern way of life are represented by Tati as 'disciplined, ascetic, mechanic, boring, absurd, and ordered'. It is not the family that inhabit the house, making it their living space, impregnating it with the family's values – but quite the opposite: they behave according to spatial rules, which are embodied in the aesthetic of the house and its machinery. To be modern means to deal with space in a particular way. The use is not inscribed in space, but rather prescribed by it. Monsieur Hulot, unable to deal with such modern machinery, and not understanding the rules (or ironically tampering with the rules), becomes a human 'glitch' in the house-machine.

In spite of all the fuss about Marc Augé's (1992) idea of non-places, he makes clear that he understands 'anthropological places' as spaces where it is possible to read inscriptions of social ties and collective history. And it is based on this definition that Augé contends that 'empirical non-places' are spaces of circulation and consumption, where social ties and collective histories find no traction – such as airports and supermarkets. However, the key element for attributing values to a portion of space is use. Use is what energizes spaces and turns them into places. Jean Baudrillard (1968) highlights use as the core of his *System of Objects*, which are fundamentally formed by the social use people make of them, beyond the technological and ideological logic of their conception and fabrication. And Lucrécia Ferrara (1986) writes that the richness of spaces emerges from the possibility of unpredictable uses. Up to this point, the construction of place relies on how perception and use of spatial features mold portions of space into places – both varying at a personal and social level. And for the unpredictable uses and changes in values, we can only accept a supermarket or an airport as an 'anthropological non-place' within a particular cultural and social framework, not as a general assumption. As I will discuss later in this book, airports can equally be considered the ultimate place, where contemporary values coalesce and shape space.

34   Constructions

Yi-Fu Tuan's works are central to the discussion of place. But it is sometimes difficult to follow the meanders of his thinking. After stating flatly that space is the same as place (1983: 58), Tuan insists on trying to define place by contrasting it with space, saying that the latter is unclear, the freedom desired by man, whereas place is security and stability (6), representing a world organized as a static concept (198). The claim that place is security and stability seems to negate its dynamic nature that arises out of use. Use changes from culture to culture and from person to person, depending on factors alien to the physical elements of space, such as psychological characteristics, purposes and beliefs – and Tuan was aware of this, emphasizing such aspects in his writings. As Maria Nieves Zedeño and Brenda Bowser (2009: 5) put it, 'people create places through behavioral interactions with nature and the supernatural', and it is based on these cognitive processes, which produce attachments to certain portions of space, that people 'motivate, structure, and transform their interactions with the material world in patterned ways'.

The attempt to define place according to assumed atavistic geographic characteristics or quantifiable and precise measurements provides constant pitfalls in the literature on place. Tuan (1983: 191) states that the city is the quintessential place; but elsewhere (Tuan, 1977; 1989) he points out that place ranges from intimate spots within each room in a house to the Earth itself, for place encompasses any portion of space to which one develops personal attachments. In this sense, it is clear that each city potentially carries meanings at least as multiple as those living in or visiting it. The city as a place includes its totality as well as its infinite twists and turns.

Saul Steinberg's cover to *The New Yorker* (29 March 1976) portrays a few bustling blocks of Manhattan from 9th Avenue towards the Hudson River; beyond the river, in one single city block he merely writes the names of Jersey City, Los Angeles and a few other cities are written on a bare desert landscape, framed by blank areas destined to Mexico and Canada; and beyond this North-American block lies the Pacific Ocean, with China, Japan and Russia written on the background. More recently, in January 2000, in another cover to *The New Yorker*, Mark Ulriksen put Manhattan at the centre and as the only celestial body in a galaxy. Inasmuch as these drawings are stereotypes, they show how New Yorkers presumably see their city as the core of the universe – at least of their universe, where their values, memories and aspirations, are materialized. New York in those examples acquires iconic values and, as such, goes beyond its materiality to represent an idea of the city.

If a ten-million-inhabitant city can be considered a singular place, what about a neighbourhood? Lynch used Beacon Hill in Boston as a well-defined neighbourhood, given that its characteristics are highly distinguished from its surroundings, with quite clear boundaries, which could make it a 'thematic unit' (Lynch 1960: 68). At the time of his writings, Beacon Hill was the object of programs aimed at raising the awareness of its importance and reinforcing its identity. Such precise and precious boundaries and distinguished features were so cherished by some planners and geographers that they became prerequisites for the characterization of neighbourhoods, and even as outlines for the design of new towns, such as those following the precepts of the New Urbanism.

Peter Weir's film 'The Truman Show' (1998) takes place in a typical new-urbanism town, with all the physical features valued for identification of a neighbourhood. In Weir's movie, written by Andrew Niccol, Truman Burbank is born and lives in a perfect city where everybody knows each other and seems to have a heartfelt sense of community. When he turns thirty, Truman finds out that strange things have been happening – from a spotlight falling down from the sky to the same people waving at him every day at the same time from the same location. Seahaven, his hometown, is completely fake, and he is the only 'real' person in a reality show.

Different from Seahaven (or the real Seaside in Florida, designed by Duany Plater-Zyberk & Company, where the film was shot) neighbourhoods do not usually have clear borders or physical features that distinctly differentiate one from another. Nor do they have homogeneous communities. They are complex, even shambolic places, with a few physical features and social practices that visitors might not identify as easily as they did in Beacon Hill.

In the late 1950s, Truman Capote opened his essay on why he had chosen to live in Brooklyn, New York, 'by choice', saying:

> Those ignorant of its allures are entitled to wonder why. For, taken as a whole, it is an uninviting community. A veritable veldt of tawdriness where even the *noms des quartiers* aggravate: Flatbush and Flushing Avenue, Bushwick, Brownsville, Red Hook. Yet, in the greenless grime-gray, oases do occur, splendid contradictions, hearty echoes of healthier days.
>
> (Capote, 2015)

The accompanying photographs, by David Attie (whose photomontage also illustrated the original publication of Capote's *Breakfast at Tiffany's*), mix beautiful seaside scenes of Brooklyn with Manhattan in the background, with ordinary street-life scenes of people talking, playing and idling on sidewalks, staircases, barber shops and ballrooms. The eye-catching images of a vague Manhattan in the background and the

36   *Constructions*

unadorned backyard scenes, the echoes of healthier days and the vibrant, unknown neighbourhood, all create some of the several unique senses of place that make Brooklyn what it is.

New York City as a whole, together with the mostly unremarkable portions of a neighbourhood within the city, fit the definition of place. Unlike space, which is immediately appropriable by our senses, place becomes a place when a portion of space is impregnated with personal or social values. As Tuan (1989: 11) puts it, places are 'mental-emotional edifices'. Hence, their dynamic richness arises out of the diverse appropriations of entities and flows by the varied and changing uses made of them by people with different ends or cultural backgrounds. Place is constructed by the process of signification, organization and hierarchizing of spatial elements through cultural substrates.

As it is now clear that cultural filters influence our perception and understanding of space, we have to put aside the belief that physical proximity determines what makes a portion of space become a place for some person or group. For example, Mecca is located geographically in Saudi Arabia, but it has a formative importance for the religion as a whole and for each Muslim individually, regardless of their geographical position. The prophet Mohammed was born in Mecca in 570 CE, where he lived and pointed the way to a single God, Allah, for people who were either polytheists or pagans. For this reason, Mecca became the central place for Muslims. Only the disciples of Mohammed enter Mecca, and only the pure enter the Great Mosque. The main building in Mecca, the Kaaba, which means 'square building', is 15 meters tall and 12 meters wide, with each vertex pointing to one of the cardinal points. The great black stone in the Kaaba pre-dates Islam and was worshipped by pagan peoples, who would kiss it and caress it to receive its power. Mohammed purified the Kaaba in the name of Allah, but Muslims retained the same ceremony and veneration. Almost two million people visit Mecca each year, following the compulsory Muslim pilgrimage for those who are able. Hundreds of millions of Muslims in all corners of the world turn towards Mecca five times a day in prayer.

As the centre place of their religion, how could one argue that the neighbourhood of a Muslim living in São Paulo or Tokyo has a more profound sense of place than Mecca, based solely in its physical proximity? Indeed, all the entities and flows that represent Mecca for a Muslim are at least as important for the constitution of their place as those they might have in their room – many of which only exist due to a non-contiguous connection in space and time with Mecca. This supports our assertion here that apprehending entities and flows, and signifying and organizing them within the concept of place in no way presupposes any physical attributes. The richness of place lies in the multifaceted process of signification, which is of a cultural rather than material order.

The impregnation of portions of space with personal or social values, that is, the construction of places, reveals ourselves to others, and especially to ourselves. Place is where memory of the past and expectation of the future come together in the present and shape the space. Two reminiscences from the explorer Wade Davis's childhood illustrate how place is simultaneously attached to memories and expectations. When Davis (2001: 16) returned to Quebec City as an adult, he writes: 'Every blade of grass resonated with a story. Shadows marked the ground where trees had fallen in my absence. Innovation and new constructions I took as personal insults, violations of something sacred that lay in the confluence of landscape and memory.' In this case, memory impregnates a portion of space and makes it his place. But Davis (2001, 17–18) tells of the first time he left Canada as a child to spend 8 weeks in Colombia, 'in the mountains above the plains, at the edge of trails that reached west to the Pacific', where

> Life was real, visceral, dense with intoxicating possibilities (...) charged with a strange intensity, a passion for life and a quiet acceptance of the frailty of the human spirit. Several of the other Canadian students longed for home. I felt as if I had finally found it.

Place is created here by expectations and values of a possible but uncertain future.

A conversation between siblings trying to describe their childhood home might shed light into hidden corners of the building. They have to be measured not in meters, but in an assortment of fantasies, monsters and fairies, fears and joys. The filtered entities and flows are sometimes disparate; and when they converge they have different meanings, forming places that seem not to fit into the same house visited many years later. Slowly the same household is reshaped, resized, resignified by siblings over the years, based on everyone's experiences of life. Post-childhood experiences redesign early-years experiences. Place is as malleable as memory.

Likewise, the same place revisited at a different time by the same person, changes dramatically – even if most of the material identifiers of the place, and the people with whom this person has shared memories of the place are still there. After returning to New Orleans to settle the sale of the family house partially destroyed by hurricane Katrina, Sarah M. Broom finishes her short story:

> I drove away before sunrise the next morning, as if possessed, completing the fourteen-hundred-mile stretch to New York without

stopping for the night, feeling that everything and absolutely nothing was behind me.

> (Sarah M. Broom, 'The Yellow House', *The New Yorker*, 24 August 2015, p. 51–5)

Estrangement from what once was called home brings us to one of the most common metaphors of place. In *La poétique de l'espace*, Gaston Bachelard (1961: 51) considers that 'rooms and houses are psychological diagrams that guide writers and poets in their analysis of intimacy'. For Bachelard, the home is a quintessential place, portions of space with the freedom to attribute meanings to entities and flows without instances of oppression determining hierarchies of value. The home would combine the protective mantle of the well known with the freedom of signification, in such a way that shared values are collectively constructed through family ties, which still leave room for the growing of personal values in the process of building each person's identity, which are also reflected in the home. In Georges Spyridaki's beautiful phrase, quoted by Bachelard (1961: 61), 'My house is diaphanous, but it is not of glass. It is more of the nature of vapor. Its walls contract and expand as I desire.'

The idea of home as an idealized place, as a protective space, has been severely questioned. First, because it would imply place as a stable singularity, rather than the multiplicity conveyed by its definition – if place is a portion of space imbued with personal or group values, it is necessarily multiple. And if different people with different values recognize their values in the same portion of space, differences naturally emerge. As Doreen Massey (1997: 320) puts it, place as a singularity, as a 'source of unproblematic identity' disfavours the concept by portraying it as 'a form of romanticized escapism from the real business of the world'.

Secondly, the experience of home can be troublesome, far from the ideal protective place. Jerry Burger (2011: 19) says that if he 'ever had doubts about the emotional bond people develop with their homes, these concerns evaporated' as soon as he started to accompany and interview people visiting their childhood homes. Regardless of whether these individuals were delighted still to find signs of their childhood in their former households, or were distressed by reliving painful memories, by visiting abusive homes, all of them were touched by their home.

Leslie Weisman's (1992) compelling book making a feminist critique of man-made social spaces, addresses the problem of violence against women in domestic settings, saying that external intervention is rare, which leads to women being trapped in a 'men's castle'. Investigating the production of the home in the United States, Joshua Price (2002) reaches a similar conclusion, stating that the idealized notion of the home as a safe place has helped to hide domestic violence against women.

Interweaving the text with testimonies of violence against women, Price (2002: 51) points out that 'Bachelard's phenomelological method is one that undermines the possibility of multivocality'. More broadly, Tim Cresswell (2004) and Shelley Mallett (2004: 74) recall that many authors have criticized Bachelard's view of the home as 'premised on the white, middle class, heterosexual nuclear family', where women are 'consigned to a life of reproductive and domestic labor' (Mallett, 2004: 75).

Victorian England celebrated the home as a 'repository for societal values' of security, repose and stability, but also 'gave rise to the cult of female domesticity' (Weisman, 1992). Women should be at home, not on the streets, 'endowed with love and gentleness, not energy and power'. Colin Ellard (2015), building on multiple authors, sees the organization of the domestic space changing notions of sexuality (when married couples had their own rooms), privacy, social roles within the family and the 'Western trend to value the individual over the group' (Ellard 2015: 62). And in a glimpse of social change, Witold Rybczynski (1992) sees the emergence of what he calls the 'androgynous home', where men, women and children redefine their roles within the household on more equal terms – although he seems to address only traditional families consisting of heterosexual parents with children.

Although these arguments against an ontological meaning of the home as a protective mantle are valid, and also if one takes home as a synonym of the household where someone spends part of his of her life, I would argue that the home as a mental model of a portion of space molded by the values of a person or a group of people is still a powerful metaphor. We must recall that Bachelard (1951) begins his book by stating that his philosophical project is dedicated to the study of the 'poetic imagination'. Home, for Bachelard, has heuristic significance in exploring the most intimate individual values if it is accepted in its uniqueness and complexity. Bachelard links the home with water and fire, elements that allow the philosopher to consider 'glimmers of reverie' that shed light on the most intimate memories, the 'immemorial' (25): the birthplace as the dreamt place, as the embodiment of a desired safe place. Bachelard was supported by the works of the psychologist Françoise Minkowska to say that even children with turbulent childhoods who depict their actual homes with similarly sombre or tempestuous traits, carry dreams of a secure place for constructing their innermost self towards the world. Finally, Bachelard (1951: 68) suggests that the future home, the dreamed home, may be 'more solid, brighter, and vaster than all past homes'.

The most primeval home is perhaps the cave. Manfredi Nicoletti begins his book on the architecture of the cave by distinguishing nature and architecture: the former has no language or signs, it simply 'is', while the latter is pure language, where even rocks are the building blocks of a

40   *Constructions*

general grammar. Nicoletti is not concerned with the occupation of natural caves, but with sculpting dwellings out of caves – either for habitation or ceremonial purposes. Sculpting rocks, turning them into meaningful spaces, signifying what is a pure state of being (nature), is an act of positioning humankind before nature. Sculpting rocks and inhabiting caves is an act of place making, which ranges from the North African Berbers to the Judeo-Christian tradition. Caves are pre-eminent in the Old Testament as places where life was engendered, revelations witnessed, and life came to an end. The *grotto* as a 'singular architectural topos' experienced a revival in the Renaissance, bearing multiple and sometimes contradictory meanings – 'sacred and profane, idyllic and bucolic, mythological and oracular' (Miller, 1982: 7). As Naomi Miller (p. 10) puts it, artificial caves are the creation of 'a cosmos in miniature, a nature that is cultivated and controlled'. Inhabiting caves is the primeval shaping of space into place, of building oneself into the world.

Heidegger highlights dwelling as an authentic existence, for which space is,

> neither an external object nor an inner experience. It is not that there are men, and over and above them space; for when I say 'a man,' and in saying this word think of a being who exists in a human manner-that is, who dwells-then by the name 'man' I already name the stay within the fourfold among thing – the fourfold being earth and heaven, divinities and mortals . . .
>
> (Heidegger 1971: 6)

Tim Cresswell (2004: 22), however, makes the point that Heidegger's selection of a farmhouse in the Black Forest to attempt to unite the spiritual and philosophical world rooted in place is 'very romantic and nostalgic', and would be much more complicated in a modern world.

Similarly romantic is the pairing of the process of individuation and the construction of one's personal space, as described in Carl Jung's (1975: 196) autobiography. Jung narrates the construction of the Tower, an endeavour he undertook when he realized that words were no longer enough: 'I needed a representation in stone of my innermost thoughts and of the knowledge I had' (Jung, 1975: 196). From selection of the site at St. Meinardtnear, Zurich, to final construction, the building stages he describes in his book reflect the process of individuation, of discovery, questioning and formation of the psychological Self. Elleman (2015: 69) analyses that Jung's notebooks give clues that the tower was a mixture of a 'life-sized version of childhood recollections', and 'events, ideas, and people of his life'.

Jung began by building a primitive cabin, with a fireplace and stone walls where the family could gather for shelter and refuge that was not just physical but also psychological. After a while it no longer expressed what he had wanted and he added an annex in the shape of a tower. Four years later the feeling of incompleteness remained. The annex was replaced by a real tower, which contained a room reserved for himself, locked with a key. Rooms were constantly added, neighbouring land acquired, some parts demolished and rebuilt, with inscriptions of ancestors' names and poems in the stone, for 'Our souls as well as our bodies are composed of individual elements which were all already present in the ranks of our ancestors' (Jung, 1975: 210).

The construction of places concerns the choice and organization of stones, rather than the stones themselves, which are united by an ethereal mixture of personal and social values. If the home is a metaphor of the social and psychological ties among those sharing a portion of space, a similar process of construction of places occurs on the urban scale. It usually happens at an ordinary level, where signs of no special interest, which would pass unnoticed by anybody living elsewhere, define the place to those living there. Doreen Massey (1997) talks about Kilburn, where she has lived for several years, and to which she has personal attachments, highlighting that although it is a peculiar place, Kilburn is far from homogeneous, rejecting a conservative view of place as having a singular and coherent identity to show that its multiple meanings to multiple people makes it a rich place, exactly because Kilburn is not one single place.

When you belong to different social circles sharing the same portion of space, the multiple meanings of place are even clearer. I write these lines at home in Cambridge, Massachusetts, equidistant from Harvard Square, MIT, and the public school my daughter attends, and a few blocks from Somerville, where an important community of Portuguese, Brazilians, and other legal and illegal migrants live. Moving from my scholarly interests to my daughter's school, our foreign friends, and switching interests and languages, makes Cambridge into my place in different ways. Knowing we will be late for school depending on who the bus driver is (not the schedule), memorizing the potholes I have to avoid on my bike when the heavy snow comes, listening to different languages (and to my own language, Portuguese, in unexpected situations), the smell of the Iranian restaurant as a landmark – all these signs build not just a landscape, but my own place as well.

The multiplicity of meanings and the ordinary elements I recognize as part of my place in Cambridge are potentially different for all the other people living here. But there are also values shared by those with common backgrounds or interests – it is quite easy here to see how college

42   Constructions

students, a strong black community, and migrants use different portions of space, making them their own places. This process usually goes unnoticed, as a peaceful overlapping of places sharing the same portion of space. But Massey (1997: 315) alerts us that a 'sentimentalized recovering of sanitized "heritages"' can be built to expel newcomers or outsiders. In this case, the sense of place, or the deliberate construction of place, becomes a reactionary process. Kay Anderson (1987: 582) analyzes that Chinatowns in many cites, and in Vancouver in particular, reveal a strong 'relationship between place, power, racial discourse, and institutional practice'. Anderson is aware that Chinese migrants were active in building their own places in the new world, and some merchants were even eager to avoid any contact with non-Chinese. Nevertheless, over time the host societies reinforced the 'Chineseness' of these neighbourhoods, and the sense of place began to be used not by those living within these areas, but by those trying to keep their inhabitants living exclusively within their limits. On a positive side, Cresswell (2004: 27) discusses how 'gay people were able to produce an affirmative vision of their own lifestyle' by occupying particular areas in West Hollywood. Attaching social values to a portion of space becomes a process of self-identification as much as a form of communicating these values with other groups.

Sometimes place acquires iconic significance by those sharing similar values and collectively experiencing the same portion of space. As a process of shared signification, meanings can be fixed to material elements through the sedimentation of social values in particular places.

This is the case of Elsinore castle, in Denmark, where Hamlet lived to avenge his father's murder by his uncle. Hamlet, a theatrical character, living in a fictional castle, transformed the real Kronborg castle in Helsingør into an iconic place in Western culture, over and above its importance to Danish culture. Kronborg is 'itself a political fact of the first order. It radiates upon the play its own stage directions. (. . .) Here, one feels, the great play has come home' (Berry, 2001: 365). In 2000, Kronborg was classified as a Unesco World Heritage site.

That is the essence of the construction of places, which is valid only if the cultural basis for the perception of these meanings is shared. You might take a vaporetto to the Lido, looking only for the beautiful Tadzio who enchanted Gustav von Aschenbach, in Thomas Mann's *Death in Venice*. You would see the Grand Hôtel de Bains, the striped changing cabins, the calm sea and imagine Tadzio running with his friends. But you would also see other tourists trampling all over it without recognizing what they are doing, for whom there will never be a silent, passionate death.

Another trap in the definition of place lies in trying to find what is genuine in it – distinguishing a 'real' place from all others. Massey (2005) recalls a common experience of many tourists travelling to Paris. They sit in a café, drink coffee and smoke, as a true Parisian experience – only to be reminded, by her inner intellectual, that neither the coffee nor the tobacco (most probably not even the waiter), are genuinely Parisian, or even French. It does not hinder the enjoyment of Paris, though. After all, taken to the extreme, there is no such thing as a genuine Paris – 200 years ago, Brillat-Savarin, the author of the *Physiology of Taste*, said 'a meal such as one can eat in Paris is a cosmopolitan whole in which every part of the world makes its appearance by way of its products'. Paris, as a place, is the overlapping of experiences, of images, of stories that make it a place in and for western culture.

Place is not secure and static in itself; rather, it is a melting pot of shifting signs attributed to entities and flows, objects and actions which pass through cultural filters, made of memories and aspirations, of values from the past and the future.

Some of these signs can be described, and this description can make other people, who do not share the same culture, recognize a portion of space as a place of the other. That is the role of tourist guides, for example. During my first months living in Quebec City, I decided to visit the same town guided by different interests. For the first weeks I took Benjamin's advice, wandering through the city like someone lost in the woods, aware of each step, the individual objects and sounds that begin to comprise a place and which would serve as a reference on future tours. Weeks later I began using a simple tourist guide, looking for streets and buildings I had not been aware of, and seeing in others important historical elements which constitute the image of Quebec portrayed to tourists, superimposing meanings on buildings I had not noticed as I passed. In this process, some places were added to the mental and affective map of the city, which had its meanings transformed.

Slowly becoming familiar with the touristic city, I knew it was also overshadowing other portions of the city that could be potential places. On long cold weekends, equipped with other guides (culinary, musical, architectural, historical) I returned to visit the same streets, the same squares – which, with additional layers of information, became other places. Places and places overlaid in the same town, which, for a while, was my town. Sometimes, exhausted by so many guides, I went out into streets that they do not include, which supposedly had no importance, but which in some cases hide places dear to my personal and emotional understanding of the city. A few years later, returning to visit the city, when I saw tourists making their own brief visits, relying on tourist guides to find which places they should visit and give importance to, I felt a

44   *Constructions*

mixture of pride and joy in knowing a Quebec they would never know, and jealousy for the moments of discovery they would have and which we usually lose when a place becomes familiar.

Place ends up being defined as a portion of space, without precise boundaries or dimensions, with meaningful elements that are reflective, that is to say meaningful for individuals or groups of people to find themselves and identify the other. The construction of places is the signifying operation that allows one to apprehend, recognize and order entities and flows, it is the unstable and fertile action responsible for creating the awareness of being in space.

The construction of territory

Place and space have been correctly considered as 'conceptual twins' (Agnew, 2012: 82). I would argue, though, that they are triplets, including territory as a third conceptual category. The definition of territory and place begins in exactly the same way: a portion of space whose entities and flows, or objects and actions, are impregnated with values reflecting the culture of a person or group. But the differences between place and territory lead to richer analysis of the manifestations of space. Indeed, restriction of the fundamental spatial categories to only two terms may lead to confusion. That is what happens with John Agnew's (2012: 84) definition of space as 'a field of practice of an area in which a group or an organization, such as a state, operates, held together in popular consciousness by a map-image and a narrative that represents it as a meaningful whole'. Agnew brings significant insights to the discussion of place and territory, drawing attention to the relationship between both – for instance, when he shows that iconic places spontaneously cherished by a community were used as symbols to reinforce the power of states (Agnew, 1989). Nonetheless, taking into account the previous discussion of the construction of space, Agnew's definition of space, equating it with the definition of territory, is extremely restrictive.

We have said that territory is a portion of space whose elements are endowed with values that reflect the culture of a person or group. In the case of the construction of place, the signifying process is centripetal, with the values coming from individuals and groups and enveloping entities and flows. A person or group projects their values on a portion of space; they see themselves reflected on it – and turn this portion of space into a place. In the case of territory the process of attributing values is centrifugal; it is a way of marking these elements with values, with the intention that any other person, entity or action that is present or occurs within this same portion of space is guided by, or even subject to the values imposed on the space. This is when values become rules. Place comes into existence when values impregnated in a portion of space are accepted by those who share them, whereas territory requires that others respect (spontaneously or not) these values and behave according to them. As with space and place, this initial definition will be refined as the chapter proceeds.

Edward Hall (1959: 45) considered territoriality as one of the ten 'Primary Message Systems', which are 'non-linguistic forms of the communication process'. Hall looked for an initial definition of territoriality in ethology. Territoriality is connected to the idea of domain, to the area of influence of a particular species over a portion of space, and over its peers. When other animals from the same species, or other species that share resources or have biological ties with the dominant species, enter that area of influence they will eventually notice this to be a region dominated by another individual or group, which controls that territory.

Territory has space as its substratum, which implies that territoriality is inscribed on certain entities and flows apprehended through sensorial and cultural filters. Therefore, the territory of a lion does not include all entities and flows pertaining to this portion of space. A gazelle that enters the portion of space dominated by the lion will be entering its territory and will be subject to it – indeed, it might be eaten – because gazelles and lions share several sensorial filters and have biological ties (both share the same ecosystem, one being a predator). But an anthill that establishes itself in this same portion of space will not be subject to the territory of the lion, because the entities and flows apprehended by both lions and ants are different to the extent that we could say they do not share the same territory.

From an anthropological point of view, Norman Ashcraft and Albert Scheflen (1976) point out that territories are formed even when space is not physically occupied, claiming that people walking in a certain direction establish a virtual territory ahead of them. Similarly, 'spaces covered by voice or gaze projection' also establish temporary territories not inscribed in the physical space (Ashcraft and Scheflen, 1976: 7), but which clearly mark personal boundaries. However intriguing, such ephemeral, intangible and highly personal territories are extremely subjective. For instance, when someone is walking along the street in a certain direction, the reason another person does not cross his/her immediate virtual path is not to avoid entering someone else's territory, but simply to avoid collision. And the reach of someone's voice is indeed a component of space, but does not establish a territory – although visiting a busy restaurant at lunchtime might persuade you otherwise.

Despite the exacerbation of their arguments, Ashcraft and Scheflen's insights point to the importance of non-physical territorial landmarks,

46 *Constructions*

which may also be built in a collective fashion – and indeed socially constructed territories are the main topic of this chapter. As Hall (1959: 51) puts it, 'the history of man's past is largely an account of his efforts to wrest from others and to defend space from outsiders.'

An important characteristic of territory, therefore, is that it is constituted provided there is a system of values shared by those occupying that portion of space. It is this system of values that determines cultural filters, and the way entities and flows must be organized to mark this portion of space in a particular way.

Another characteristic, also with roots in biology, is that territorial domination is more accentuated at the centre and becomes more rarefied towards the periphery. However, when considering this as a foundation for the concept of territory, it needs to be clear that the portion of space called territory does not necessarily cover a continuous geographical area. Take the Roman Catholic religion: all the world's Catholics are part of the territory whose influence emanates from the Vatican. But as we have seen, only those who share the same values, which are projected on entities and flows, are subject to the territory. In other words, although Kosovo is geographically closer than Brazil to the Vatican, Kosovo Muslims are not included in the Catholic territory centred on Rome, while Brazilian Catholics are.

Robert Sack (1986) defines territoriality as 'a strategy to establish different degrees of access to people, things, and relationships' (20), whose purpose is 'an attempt by individuals or groups to affect the interactions of others' (30). Broadly, territory is a device designed to control resources (Brighenti, 2010: 62). Territoriality is thus a form of dominion or management of a certain area, where contiguity between the elements of a portion of space is not essential. Nonetheless, in many cases those who organize and dominate a territory pursue physical contiguity. Again, religious territories are a good example, and conversion, sometimes forced, has been used as a way of making people subject to a particular territory. The Catholic Inquisition had a violent conversion program, punishing individuals for ideas opposed to its canon, when these ideas were aired in a portion of space that the Church considered to be its own territory.

We have used Edgar Alan Poe's short story 'The Pit and the Pendulum' to discuss space. We can use the continuation of the same story to discuss territory – and show how one can be turned into the other. After being judged and condemned to death, the narrator loses consciousness and is placed in a dark cell. On awakening he can see nothing (and he is actually afraid of what he could be seeing) and starts to explore the space through his immediate senses: touch, hearing and hesitant movements. While still cautiously trying to discover the space, 'there came thronging upon my recollection a thousand vague rumours of the horrors of Toledo'. As soon as he remembers the name of the city, and the reader reads it, we realize that he is incarcerated in a prison of the Spanish Inquisition, and that the narrator's cell is subject to the territory of the Catholic Church. And we also recall the measures the Church used to take to ensure domination of its 'territory' over people, objects and actions: a set of symbols, ideas, and rituals – and the banishment of others. From apprehending his cell through touch to realizing he was in Toledo, his initial sensory perception of space acquires a layer of meaning, which makes this portion of space part of a larger territory.

With these examples I intend to argue that, like place, territory is not a rigid demarcation of a portion of space. Rather, its construction is determined by how people or social groups appropriate space at different scales with different interests and within different timeframes. Territory, like space, and place, becomes a powerful analytical tool – leading Andrea Brighenti (2010: 55) to coin the term 'territoriology' for the scientific study of territories.

The construction of territories as semiotic devices, which can explain and establish control of a portion of space, involves the overlapping of interconnected physical, social and symbolic layers, which may be expressed through borders, laws and national anthems, for instance.

In order to be accepted by different social groups living in the same portion of space, common practices and rules are established. Those living in a territory, even temporarily, are subject to its rules and practices, which are enforced by institutions (a set of formal and informal protocols). The legitimacy of territory depends on recognition of its rules and institutions by social groups living in other territories as well. The rules of two territories can be completely different, even antagonistic towards each other; but they must be mutually recognized as legitimate in order to make a portion of space into a territory.

The most institutionalized form of territory lies in the idea of the State. City-states submitted their inhabitants to laws that governed life in particular portions of space. Lewis Mumford identifies the Greek city as revolutionary in history because it was formed not through the enlargement of a settlement, but by attracting country dwellers to the polis, in search of opportunities and security. Cities were where they could find 'freedom and openness of mind' (Mumford, 1982: 148). The Greek city provided security not through walls, but through values cherished by its citizens. The territory of these cities was supported by a contradiction, however: on the one hand a certain freedom of action, protection of inhabitants and diversity of cultures; and on the other hand, violence: the Greek city 'imposed a drastic system of compulsion and regimentation' (Mumford, 1982: 56). This is an important feature of

48   *Constructions*

territory: any element that is under its influence is expected to be subject to it. Laws and orders are equally responsible for the security provided by the city and for the repression of any act against the territory of the polis.

Boundaries are one of the most common non-human actors of a territory. Boundaries are not simply a separation of one element from the other. As a device, boundaries are designed to separate entities, or to control which flows can move, when, from and to where, with what frequency. Simplistic and impermeable boundaries are those that block flows. As a territorial device, boundaries work selectively, determining which flows and entities can communicate with each other. Boundaries may be ephemeral and flexible. Their stability and hardness vary throughout history. Stuart Elden (2004: 85), building on Foucault and Heidegger, stresses the understanding of boundaries as a sign of transition, not enclosure. Nevertheless, when Elden discusses the territorial implications of the 'War on Terror' – a set of security measures led by the United States and adopted by several countries after the terrorist attack in New York on 11 September 2001 – he sees the challenge to threats of combat as not being tied to the precise territories of nation states. 'In face of this deterritorialization, there must therefore be a reterritorialization of the power of the state. Borders need to be protected, reinforced, or erected, and the apparatus of the state takes on an even more significant role' (Elden, 2009: 11).

At the beginning of the expansion of Christianity in Europe, parishes, its religious territories, had no legitimacy to anyone outside the Church. Over the centuries, they became territorial devices incorporated by kingdoms to legitimate their power over a portion of space, as a way of exerting control over populations, tying together religious and secular beliefs and rules. Church and state amalgamated themselves into territorial machines.

Although clear boundaries are not prerequisites of territories – there are no boundaries defining Berber nomadic territories in northern Africa, although other tribes recognize them – boundaries are a semiotic device that distinguishes territory from space and place. Territory is not necessarily a bounded space; but territorial forces definitely tend to bound space, and for this reason boundaries are a critical device of territory – even when they are fluid or unclear.

Deleuze and Guattari (2010) in their treatise on *nomadology* present a powerful idea of the nomad as an agent of deterritorialization, someone for whom boundaries do not exist. They oppose sedentary space with nomadic space. The former is 'striated', enclosed and well defined, whereas the latter is 'smooth', whose 'traits' are erased by the nomad's trajectories. Without clear, strong, or permanent marks, the nomad 'does not move' (45) for his is a homogeneous space. Nomads 'add desert to desert, steppe to steppe' (46).

However potent and heuristic the nomadic figure has become in recent decades as a metaphor ranging from the urban homeless to global businesspeople, Deleuze and Guattari's historical bases have been questioned as marked by orientalism, which presents the Orient – mainly the Near East and Arab world originally discussed by Edward Said – through the eyes of the Occident. Christopher Miller's (1993) critique of Deleuze and Guattari is that their nomad is based on colonial ethnographic sources. The risk would be on the one hand the romanticization of the nomad, and on the other hand a prejudicial view of the nomad's world.

Nomads are people of the desert. Deserts are frequently depicted as immense areas devoid of signs of life. Deserts are both fascinating and threatening. They are vast. And their expanses seem homogeneous, without clear spatial hierarchies, paths or boundaries. But this vastness and homogeneity are characteristics of an imagery of the desert produced by Western eyes. As Inge Boer (2006: 33) puts it, 'The invisibility of boundaries keeps us from apprehending the very conditions in which nomads live'; adding that 'nomads know not only how to read invisible maps, but also know that mapping invisible maps into visible ones went hand in hand with colonialism and struggles over the uncertain territories around which boundaries were drawn.'

Space and place are essentially boundless, whereas the epitomic territory has clear demarcations. Understood in this context, the nomad is a figure that transits across well established boundaries, but also who apprehends boundaries not easily grasped by sedentary eyes. Boundaries influence behavioural patterns (Newman, 2003) for those who are inside, outside and crossing them. And this situational position in relation to boundaries is what defines and makes visible the territorial characteristic of flows of people, things and ideas (Brighenti, 2010).

Physical boundaries are the most obvious device for demarcating a territory. But even without walls, the limits of city-states were well enough defined for constant conflict to exist between them. From their core, city-states established areas of influence that defined allegiance to the central power, commercial exchange and military outreach. The influence of one city-state upon a portion of space also determined who were considered as its citizens, those who were subject to its laws and therefore received protection. In a mixture of subservience and loyalty, one of the most severe penalties for inhabitants who disobeyed the laws of the city-state was exile. When Romeo Montague is accused of the murder of Juliet Capulet's cousin in William Shakespeare's *Romeo and Juliet*, his punishment is expulsion from Verona.

50 *Constructions*

> *Friar Laurence*: A gentler judgment vanish'd from his lips,
> Not body's death, but body's banishment.
> *Romeo*: Ha! banishment! be merciful, say 'death;'
> For exile hath more terror in his look,
> Much more than death: do not say 'banishment.'
> *Friar Laurence*: Hence from Verona art thou banished.
> Be patient, for the world is broad and wide.
> *Romeo*: There is no world without Verona walls,
> But purgatory, torture, hell itself.
>
> (William Shakespeare, *Romeo and Juliet*, Act III,
> Scene III. The Oxford Shakespeare, 1914)

For Romeo, exile means not just distance from Juliet but also loss of citizenship, loss of his identity. If not in Verona, where could he go? Verona is his territory – not because Romeo is responsible for its territorial organization, or because he has some power over it. He does not. Verona is Romeo's territory because he accepts the values that characterize this territory, and because its peers accept him in it. A mixture of subservience and loyalty, of identification with rules and values that determines the way one lives in a portion of space that, slowly, becomes the person's own values.

Geopolitical borders do not necessarily coincide with geographical features. Even knowing that the drawing of these borders concerns the relationships between geography and history, the precise demarcation of the territory is in itself part of modern history. It is not possible to trace with any precision the territorial boundaries of the indigenous peoples who occupied what is now America or Africa. Of course they all had their territories, in which their values were valid and which they defended from invaders. The key point here is that the precise demarcation of the territory of a nation state is an instrument for administration of a particular portion of space, characteristic of its construction, just like the other symbols, such as language or currency. For David Harvey (2001: 213), 'the process of state formation was, and still is, dependent upon the creation of certain kinds of geographical understandings (everything from mapping boundaries to the cultivation of some sense of national identity within those boundaries'.

The power of boundaries serves to control those living within them, and is a device to protect the territory from those living and acting outside it. Boundaries bring with them a double suspicion: those who are bounded must watch for their acts, for they are walled – at the extreme, every way out is under surveillance; and those who are outside these boundaries are considered *a priori* conveyors of disturbance. Michel Maffesoli (1997) writes about the Sophists of ancient Greece as the first cosmopolitans, travelling from city to city, promoting the exchange of ideas and the consequent cultural enrichment of the places they visited. But Plato considered them 'birds of passage', and advised that they should be welcomed, but outside the cities. Once accepted within the city, they should subject themselves to its territory and its rules; but they were not supposed to be considered as belonging to the city. To be considered a citizen would imply the construction of an identity. It means that the individuals living in a particular territory are not only subject to its rules, but ideally also accept them as part of the territorial identity, and would identify themselves with the values attributed to particular objects and actions. Romeo had no command over Verona, but the city was his place and his territory, in which he saw himself and others who shared the same cultural characteristics, as parts of a collective identity. In this case, the centrifugal characteristic of a territory, in which values rise from the centre and propagate over a portion of space, determining the behaviour of flows and entities, is turned into the centripetal characteristic of place, in which people project their personal or group values onto portions of space. It is not unusual to see the amalgamation of territorialities with a sense of place. Romeo considers Verona as his place, whereas for the city-state of Verona he is nothing but a subject of this territory.

Therefore, although we must feel ourselves belonging to a territory, and call it our place (such as the home country), one must not be fooled: most socially-constructed territories, such as a nation state, are artificially shaped through symbolic values, which are impregnated in a portion of space through symbols, rituals, language and morals, which determine the appropriate behaviour expected of their citizens. This social behaviour, in a cycle, reinforces people's behaviour, reinstating the territory as the rightful way of appropriating that portion of space.

As we have seen in the case of Romeo, territory and place were almost interchangeable concepts, with people taking values that were actually crafted by those controlling a portion of space as their own or belonging to a group; a mixture of subservience and identity, as discussed before. In these cases, the idea of nation is similar to that of motherland. It is the portion of the shared space that serves as an 'archive of fond memories' (Tuan, 1983: 171).

Building a cultural identity for a territory is therefore a strategic device for those who wish for control over a portion of space, which can be done subtly or drastically. The goal is to confound subservience with identity and loyalty, the former a feature of territory, the latter of place. North Korea is a dramatic contemporary example of how despots try to craft loyalty out of subservience, identity out of subjection. The country keeps its population quarantined within its over-controlled borders, uses 'symbol and ritual among its many extremes of political and cultural

52   Constructions

practice' (Mediclott, 2005: 70), and carefully choreographs all contact with the external world, either through television broadcasts or rare foreign visits, to reinstate the symbolism of North Korean identity.

Territories take multiple forms. All of them share the appropriation of portions of space through some form of control. The Greek 'democracy' was exclusive to landowners. The ownership of a portion of space is still a socially designed device that legitimatizes those who belong to a territory, and those who are merely subject to a territory. Bertrand Badie (1995) points out that this scattered territorial appropriation was first established in modern Europe, Africa, the Middle East and Far East alike. The state did not have hegemonic control over a certain space, but instead controlled portions of space through extreme fragmentation of an area, each fragment constituting a small territory. A different situation is found in the territorial notion of empire. The empire builds an identity that is intended to be universal, in which the identities of minorities are accepted as long as they do not oppose the centre. That was the view of the Holy Roman Empire. The power of empires lay in the capacity to control and subject societies to a centre, without being based on precise boundaries, blood ties or homogeneous culture. There are core values, and oftentimes a pledge of allegiance to territorial lords. For daily activities, languages, cultural and religious practices, there could be multiple territories and an infinite number of groups who identified particular portions of space as their place, without any direct or symbolic control from the centre of the empire. People felt they were simultaneously Neapolitan and Roman, Briton and Roman, African and Roman.

The nineteenth century brought a stricter way of defining and managing territories. The centre of an empire, or a state, as the source of values that would spread over a portion of space found a more powerful territorial device: geopolitical boundaries. The transformation of territory as based on sociocultural values into a political-territorial entity has infected more and more people throughout the world (Tuan, 1983: 195). Paul Claval (1993) sees that the scales (including ideologies) of identification with a portion of space change in this transformation, but the role of territoriality in structuring society is again confirmed. And despite hasty analyses of globalizing forces shattering international borders, global menaces such as terrorist attacks by transnational groups are leading to the reinforcement of borders (Elden, 2009). Boundaries are still one of the most efficient devices for exerting control over a portion of space and managing its people, entities and flows.

The idea of the nation state tends to be based on a cultural substrate as close as possible to the hegemonic inhabitants of a portion of space.

Likewise, the builders of nation states also anchor their legitimacy in their aspirations. As Yim (1980) shows in the case of North Korea, for example, its leaders claim they are the genuine representatives of the Korean people, for its language is not tainted by foreign words as in South Korea, but on the other hand its leaders have purified the language, eliminating Chinese characters, and calling on linguists to coin 'scientific and technical words'. Thus, in terms of language, a balance of heritage and future endorses the symbolic power of the Kim family in North Korea.

The modern nation state implied the constitution of a territory with precise boundaries, within which values, rules and forms of organization must be subject to a central control, and whose legitimacy depends on all other nation states respecting the ruling system within these boundaries.

In an atlas of the modern world, nation states are connected to languages, religions, currencies and flags. However, it was (and still is) rare for all the inhabitants of a defined portion of space to have a shared language or religion at the moment when it was transformed into a nation state. In France, like several other European countries, the national language was imposed to the detriment of various others, which were abolished or treated as dialects. The same happened with religion. In many cases other languages and religions were permitted but not considered official; that is, they did not enter into the national canon and became anomalous to the core characteristics of the identity of that national territory. Flags are the quintessential symbols of a nation state, with colours, designs and slogans representing certain values that have to be accepted as characteristic of that territory – without necessarily corresponding to the experience of those living in the space defined by such territory.

During the nineteenth and twentieth centuries, the organization of international relations was reshaped by the common denominator of the nation state. Nation states encompass most of the world's population. Nation states reinforce the notion that the limits of state power coincide with the limits of state territory, with states as 'fixed units of sovereign space' (Agnew, 1994) – as if territorial states existed prior to the society that formed them, dehistoricizing their formative processes. Stuart Elden (2009: 171) points out that territorial sovereignty happens at the intersection of terror and territory: sovereign states, 'are able to exercise a violence within their territory that they claim is legitimate. Those who are deemed not to have a sovereign state – non-state organizations, national self-determination movements and individuals – are in a different position. Their violence is seen as illegitimate by definition, as "terror" '.

54   Constructions

Agnew (1994) refers to the prerogative that state sovereignty coincides with a demarcated territory as a 'territorial trap'. On the one hand, it justifies eradication of the power of intermediated groups; and on the other hand the enforcement of territorial rules can be made through different forms of alliances between territories – involving military treaties, monetary regimes and so on. This idea seems to tie in with Joe Painter's (2010) notion of the 'plasticity of state spatiality', where territorial configurations would be formed outside modernistic state territorialities.

Beyond rules and boundaries, territories rely on non-official symbols that were supposed to represent shared values, and thus unite those living within their limits and under their rules. This is the story of Romantic Germany and the Muralists in Mexico. Symbols are artificial signs intended to represent something not by retaining its characteristics, but by interposing a sign that is in itself completely alien to the object's (or phenomenon's) characteristics. Symbols represent something by collective agreement, not by analogy. A picture of Mount Fuji is an icon of the mountain, for it tries to retain its characteristics – anyone who has seen the mountain and sees a picture of it will recognize it. On the other hand, 富士山 only represents the mountain to those who read Japanese. In the case of nation states, symbols are constructed to condense the cultural, social and political representation of a territory. Moreover, they are designed to create 'one' national culture, a set of national values and habits that would unify all the individuals in a territory. A classic example would be modern France, whose Legislative Assembly decreed in 1792 that an altar to the fatherland should be erected in all cities, which included the Declaration of Human Rights and the phrase 'the citizen is born, lives and dies for the fatherland'. Or there is the totalitarian nationalism of Adolf Hitler, whose Nazi party used ancestral ethnic signs like the swastika, found among ancient Basque and Nordic peoples, in an attempt to reframe Germany's identity (Satanyano, 1994: 323).

The search for cultural unity requires the overcoming (or suppression) of local differences. Basques and Catalans become Spanish, Quebecois become Canadians – even if they have different languages and histories, they still struggle for acceptance of their language and histories as part of the nation state that is above them. This is because the nation state is the territorial system accepted by peer nation states, which have built militarily and economically powerful international institutions based on this logic.

As an artificial device, the nation state creates mechanisms that enable (or persuade) the inhabitants of the portion of space under its aegis to feel identified with it – as Tuan wrote (1983: 195), making the nation state seem like 'a concrete place – not just a political idea – to which people could feel deep attachment'.

This attribution of meanings to entities, flows and signs of a portion of space, making them strong enough to govern any other elements, is a feature of territory. The fixing of a meaning to an element is in turn essential to the construction of symbols, which reinforces the ties between symbols and territories.

Perhaps because they are much more fixed to the physical space than language or anthems, geographical boundaries seem to be inherent to territory. Although imprecise, shifting over time or malleable, boundaries are a key feature of territory. They help to differentiate insiders from outsiders; who belong to each portion of space and who does not. A person or a group are partially defined, and define themselves, in relation to their position within boundaries, or which borders they are allowed to cross (Newman, 2003: 277).

Modern maps are based on boundary lines that sharply distinguish one portion of space from the other. In the many contradictions of his thinking, Yi-Fu Tuan (1983: 137) considers at one point that maps are essentially ahistorical, since they do not assume any 'reordering of time as well as of space', as if they represented portions of space defined in and by themselves. Further on in the same book he writes that cartography can be used for political ends (197). Clearly his second claim seems to capture better the symbolic and historical importance behind the drawing of maps. Maps are 'images with historically specific codes' (Harley, 2009: 129), which are defined and depicted as a form of controlling a territory. Maps are a discourse about a portion of space. By selecting specific features of a portion of space, organizing and representing them in a certain way, maps intend to convey the message of how a portion of space should be organized. Who draws the boundaries, for what purposes and for whom, become the underlying questions in cartographic analysis (Brighenti, 2010). Thus, maps are symbolic devices designed to reinstate a territory.

The nineteenth and twentieth centuries saw alterations to the map of Europe several times. These changes in European cartography reflect political shifts as well as cultural, economic, linguistic and religious ones. A map is one representation of territory, and like any representation, it is dynamic, constructed and reconstructed over time. Sometimes cartographic representations reflect these changes, but sometimes they foster these changes – that is, are used as instruments to trigger transformations, and to drive them into a specific direction. As J Brian Harley (2009: 132) puts it, 'As much as guns and warships, maps have been the weapons of imperialism.'

56   Constructions

Bertrand Badie (1995: 20–21) refers to the Persian or Ottoman empires, which assumed a universalizing territoriality while at the same time not crushing other cultures or retaining their particular spaces of identity. In Badie's example of the Kurds, their conflicts with a State began with the modern demarcation of territory, particularly with the definition of a Turkish nation state, which besides seeking to erase Kurdish territory also divided it between other national states. Cartography is an ideological representation of the state of the world, and its alterations are evidence of that dynamic.

Internal territorialities within a city usually have no precise boundaries. They exist under a municipal territory. But ethnically predominant areas within the city mix a sense of place with subtle demarcation of territories. As places, each group identifies itself with a portion of space in the city – where they see their values reflected on entities and flows, on objects and actions, and on themselves. As territories, invisible lines are often drawn; lines that determine who is allowed to enter or stay in specific areas, where members of each group might feel safe. These invisible lines have no power of jurisdiction, but they define strong social boundaries.

Slums in several developing countries constitute territories within the urban fabric of big cities. Their populations share values and tacit rules that are enforced by community leaders. Sometimes the community slowly creates these values and rules, at other times they are overseen by drug dealers. Although those living inside and outside the slums recognize their territories, there are often no clear limits separating them from the surrounding formal city. In a mixture of contempt for their situation, the difficulty of dealing with the social issues they represent, or even fear to enter these informal territories, the presence of the state amounts to nothing. Some slums become almost autonomous territories within the city, with the tacit agreement of the official state.

The formation of the nation state can be said to require a policy of crushing or destruction of the vigor of a place (the space of identity experienced in everyday life) in favour of the construction of a territory, whose symbols of identity are also devices for controlling the everyday life of those living under its influence. In short, place is closer to experience, while territory is fundamentally symbolic. In the process of apprehending and understanding a particular setting, Lucrécia Ferrara (1993: 19) identifies three basic operations: perception, reading and interpretation. We might say that territory is constructed to favour interpretation. Perception is the process through which the entities and flows that constitute the perceived space are apprehended: reading is the organization and hierarchization of these elements so that the individual can find himself/herself (his or her cultural measures) in relation to these elements; and interpretation occurs when those elements are reorganized in a way that their characteristics are not only relevant but also have special meanings attached to them, to become a vehicle for transmitting a particular worldview to those using it.

Jean Baudrillard (1968) shows how everyday industrial utensils, produced in series to function always in the same manner, quite often encounter unforeseen uses that subvert those planned by the designers. And we have discussed the example of Monsieur Hulot, Jacques Tati's character who deconstructs the over-organized modernist house. Nonetheless, he agrees from the outset that the design of these objects contains a latent ideological charge. So technological development enhances territorial scope separate from geographical contiguity. Considering the modern territories of nation states, several authors (Marshall McLuhan is an insightful reference here) have written about the role of the alphabet and the printing press as an example of the expansion of the area of influence of a particular culture. The production of numerous books from the same block revolutionized the transmission of written knowledge, previously the stronghold of copyists. On the one hand, the dissemination of the printed word led to the favouring of a restricted number of written languages that would facilitate the use of a large-scale production technique – and dismiss languages spoken by few people. On the other hand, the printing press was able to spread the word of the Catholic Church more widely than the oral language (in Latin) with which it made contact with the population. Thus, the printing press enabled the implementation of official national languages, and slowly caused the elimination of local languages. However much a king or prince established an official language in his territory, while communication was essentially spoken, ideological control would be difficult, even insignificant. The printing press propelled the widespread dissemination of a particular language chosen and imposed as official. It also enabled the publication and enforcement of the laws governing that territory.

Territory, particularly in the modern world, is a conceptual device and an instrument designed for managing a portion of space, and the objects, people, and actions within it. Territory tends to have boundaries, which are respected internally and externally; and its construction includes symbolic and cultural elements that are used as identification markers of this portion of space, as well as common denominators for the relationships between people.

In this chapter I have defined space, place and territory as singular but interrelated concepts. The differences between them are not of scale, intensity or discipline. They are conceptually distinct; and their distinctiveness retains their conceptual strength. But they are interdependent; and likewise, their interdependence retains their conceptual strength. After having constructed each concept separately, in the next chapter

58   Constructions

I explore the concordant and conflictive relations between space, place and territory. Having each concept clearly defined, it is time to put them in contact with each other. It is time for the conceptual enactment of space, place and territory.

References

Agnew, John (1989) "The devaluation of place in social science". In: Agnew, John; Duncan, James (eds) *The power of place*. Boston, MA: Unwin Hyman, 9–29.

Agnew, John (1994) The territorial trap: The geographical assumptions of international relations theory. *Review of International Political Economy*, 1(1): 53–80.

Agnew, John (2012) "Space: place". In: Cloke, Paul; Johnston, Ron (eds) *Spaces of geographical thought*. London: Sage, 82–96.

Anderson, Kay (1987) The idea of chinatown: The power of place and institutional practice in the making of a racial category. *Annals of the Association of American Geographers*, 77(4): 580–598.

Ashcraft, Norman; Scheflen, Albert (1976) *People space*. Garden City, NY: Anchor.

Augé, Marc (1992) *Non-Lieux. Introduction à une anthropologie de la surmodernité*. Paris: Seuil.

Bachelard, Gaston (1961) *La poétique de l'espace*. Paris: Presses Universitaire de France (© 1957).

Berry, Ralph (2001) Hamlet's Elsinore revisited. *Contemporary Review*, 279(1631): 362–366.

Boer, Inge (2006) *Uncertain territories*. Amsterdam: Rodopi.

Bollnow, Otto F. (2011) *Human space*. London: Hyphen (© 1963).

Brighenti, Andrea (2010) New media and the prolongations of urban environments. *Convergence: The International Journal of Research into New Media Technologies* 16: 471–487.

Brockman, John (1986) *Einstein, Gertrude Stein, Wittgenstein & Frankenstein: Re-inventing the universe*. New York, NY: Viking.

Burger, Jerry (2011) *Returning home*. Plymouth: Rowman & Littlefield.

Capote, Truman (2015) *Brooklyn: A personal memoir – with the lost photographs of David Attie*. New York, NY: The Little Bookroom.

Casey, Edward (1993) *Getting back into place: Toward a renewed understanding of the place-world*. Indianapolis, IN: Indiana University Press.

Castells, Manuel (2014) Talk at the Harvard Graduate School of Design, February 18.

Casti, John (1997) *Would-be worlds*. New York, NY: John Wiley & Sons.

Crang, Mike (2005) "Time: Space". In: Cloke, Paul; Johnston, Ron (eds) *Spaces of geographical thought*. London: Sage, 198–220.

Cresswell, Tim (2004) *Place: A short introduction*. Malden, MA: Blackwell.

DaMatta, Roberto (1991) *A casa e a rua: Espaço, cidadania, mulher e morte no Brasil*. Rio de Janeiro: Guanabara Koogan.

Davis, Wade (2001) *Light at the edge of the world*. Vancouver: Douglas & McIntyre.

Deleuze, Gilles; Guattari, Félix (2010) *Nomadology: The war machine*. Seattle, WA: Wormwood (originally appeared in *A thousand plateaus*, Translated by Brian Massumi).

Derrida, Jacques (1993) *Khôra*. Paris: Galilée.

Elden, Stuart (2001) *Mapping the present: Heidegger, Foucault and the project of a spatial history*. London: Continuum.

Elden, Stuart (2004) *Understanding Lefebvre*. London: Continuum.

Elden, Stuart (2009) *Terror and territory*. Minneapolis, MN: University of Minnesota Press.

Ellard, Colin (2015) *Place of the heart: The psychogreography of everyday life*. New York, NY: Bellevue Literary Press.

Emmorey, Karen (2004) "Language and space". In: Penz, François; Radick, Gregory; Howell, Robert. *Space in science, art and society*. Cambridge: Cambridge University Press, 22–45.

Foucault, Michel (1986) Of other spaces: Utopias and heterotopias. *Diacritics*, 16(1): 22–27.

Gehl, Jan (2010) *Cities for people*. Washington, DC: Island Press.

Hall, Edward (1959) *The silent language*. Greenwich, Connecticut: Fawcett Premier.

Hall, Edward (1966) *The hidden dimension*. New York, NY: Doubleday.

Harley, Brian J (2009) "Maps, knowledge, and power". In: Henderson, George; Waterstone, Marvin (eds) *Geographic thought: A praxis perspective*. London: Routledge, 129–148.

Harvey, David (2001) *Spaces of capital*. Edinburgh: Edinburgh University Press.

Heidegger, Martin (1971) "Building dwelling thinking". In: *Poetry, language, thought*. New York, NY: Harper Colophon (Translated by Albert Hofstadter).

Herzog, Werner (1974) *The Enigma of Kaspar Hauser – Film*. West Germany: Filmverlag der Autoren ZDF.

Hirt, Irène (2012) Mapping dreams/dreaming maps: Bridging indigenous and western geographical knowledge. *Cartographica, 47*(2): 105–120.

Hoffman, Jeffrey (2004) "Exploring space". In: Penz, François; Radick, Gregory; Howell, Robert (eds) *Space in science, art and society*. Cambridge: Cambridge University Press, 150–171.

Kido, Ewa (2012) Elements of the urbanscape in Tokyo. *Teka Komisji Architektury, Urbanistyki i Studiów Krajobrazowych O.L. PAN, 8*(1): 75–92.

Koslofsky, Craig (2011) *Evening's empire*. Cambridge: Cambridge University Press.

Kraftl, Peter; Horton, John (2008) Space of every-night life: for geographies of sleep, sleeping and sleepiness. *Progress in human geography, 32*(4): 509–524.

Lefebvre, Henri (1981) *La production de l'espace*. Paris: Anthropos (© 1974).

Leibniz, Gottfried Wilhelm (1995) *Philosophical writings* (edited by G H R Parkinson). London: Everyman (© 1715).

Lilley, Keith (2014) *City and cosmos: The medieval world in urban form*. London: Reaktion.

Lynch, Kevin (1960) *The image of the city*. Cambridge, MA: MIT Press.

Lynch, Kevin (1990) "Reconsidering *The image of the city*". In: *City sense and city design: Writings and projects of Kevin Lynch* (edited by Tridib Banerjee; Michael Southworth). Cambridge, MA: MIT Press.

60 *Constructions*

Maffesoli, Michel (1997) *Du Nomadisme. Vagabondages initiatiques.* Paris: Livres de Poche.

Mallett, Shelley (2004) Understanding home: A critical review of the literature. *The Sociological Review,* 52(1): 62–89.

Marejko, Jan (1994) *Dix méditations sur l'espace et le mouvement.* Lausanne: L'âge d'homme.

Martouzet, Denis; Laffont, Georges-Henry (2012) Tati, théoricien de l'urbain et Hulot, habitant. *L'Espace Géographique,* 39: 159–171.

Massey, Doreen (1997) "A global sense of place". In: Barnes, Trevor; Gregory, Derek (eds) *Reading human geography.* London: Arnold, 315–323.

Massey, Doren (2005) *For space.* London: Sage.

McLuhan, Marshall (1964) *Understanding media: The extensions of man.* New York, NY: McGraw Hill.

Mediclott, Carol (2005) Symbol and sovereignty in North Korea. *SAIS Review of International Affairs,* 25(2): 69–79.

Miller, Naomi (1982) *Heavenly caves. Reflections on the garden grotto.* New York, NY: Georges Braziller.

Nicoletti, Manfredi (1980) *L'architettura delle caverne.* Roma: Laterza.

Pavić, Milorad (1988) *Dictionary of the khazars: A lexicon novel.* New York, NY: Knopf (© 1984).

Plato (2000). *Timaeus and Critias.* Mineola, NY: Dover Thrift (Translated by B Jowett).

Poe, Edgar A (1850) "The pit and the pendulum". In: *The works of the late Edgar Allan Poe* (Vol I). New York, NY: J. S. Redfield, Clinton Hall, pp. 310–324.

Price, Joshua (2002) The apotheosis of home and the maintenance of spaces of violence. *Hypatia,* 17(4), 39–70. DOI: 10.1111/j.1527-2001.2002.tb01073.x

Rybczynski, Witold (1992) *Looking around: Aa journey through architecture.* New York, NY: Viking.

Rykwert, Joseph (1976) *The idea of town.* Princeton, NJ: Princeton University Press.

Sack, Robert (1986) *Human territoriality: Its theory and history.* Cambridge: Cambridge University Press.

Sagan, Carl (1997) *Billions and billions.* New York, NY: Ballantine.

Santos, Milton (1979) *Espaço e Sociedade.* Petrópolis: Vozes.

Santos, Milton (1990) *Espace et Méthode.* Paris: Publisud.

Schimd, Christian (2008) "Henri Lefebvre's theory of the production of space". In: Goonewardena, Kanishka; Kipfer, Stefan; Milgrom, Richard; Schimd, Christian (eds) *Space, difference, everyday life.* London: Routledge, 27–45.

Shields, Rob (2013) *Spatial questions.* London: Sage.

Siegfried, André (1947) "Quelques aspects mal explorés de la géographie: la géographie des couleurs, des odeurs et des son". Conférence donnée à Paris le 18 mars 1947. In: Dulau, Robert; Pitte, Jean-Robert (eds). Géographie des odeurs. Paris et Montréal, L'Harmattan, 1998.

Stanek, Lukasz (2011) *Henri Lefebvre on space. Architecture, urban research, and the production of theory.* Minneapolis, MN: University of Minnesota Press.

Süskind, Patrick (1986) *Perfume: The story of a murderer.* New York, NY: Vintage.

Tschumi, Bernard (1994) *Architecture & disjunction.* Cambridge, MA: MIT Press.

Tuan, Yi-Fu (1989) "A sense of place". In: Schoff, Grethcen; Tuan, Yi-Fu (eds) *Two essays on a sense of place*. Madison: Wisconsin Humanities Committee.

Tuan, Yi-Fu (1977) *Space and place: The perspective of experience*. Minneapolis, MN: University of Minnesota Press.

Ueda, Hirofumi (2014) "Landscape perception in Germany and Japan". In: Shimizu, Hiroyuki; Murayama, Akito (eds) *Basic and clinical environmental approaches in landscape planning*. Tokyo: Springer, 15–24.

Virilio, Paul (1997) *Open sky*. London: Verso *(La vitesse the liberation)*.

Walser, Robert (2015) *Looking at pictures*. New York, NY: Christine Burgin and New Directions.

Weisman, Leslie (1992) *Discrimination by design. A feminist critique of the man-made environment*. Chicago, IL: University of Illinois Press.

Whyte, William (1984) *The social life of small urban spaces* [video recording]. New York, NY: Municipal Art Society of New York.

Yim, Yong Soon (1980) Language reform as a political symbol in North Korea. *World Affairs*, 142(3): 216–236.

Zedeño, Maria Nieves; Bowser, Brenda (2009) *The archaeology of meaningful places*. Salt Lake City, UT: University of Utah Press.

3 The enactment of space, place and territory

Space, place and territory are unique concepts. They do share the same core definition, which is the space, formed by the relationships between entities and flows screened by sensorial and cultural filters. As the definitions of both place and territory begin by stating they are a portion of space imbued with the values of a person or a group, they are often treated interchangeably. Nevertheless, the distinction between them is both epistemological and methodological. Their singularity is what makes them tools to understand the different manifestations of spatial phenomena. Treating them interchangeably hampers more refine analysis of how persons and social groups use and appropriate portions of space. Treating them as opposite denies their common conceptual core. It is by maintaining and reaffirming their commonalities and at the same time highlighting their differences that we can shed light in complex spatial configurations.

Another aspect to take into consideration is that any use of these concepts is embedded in the culture of a period – or from a broader view, they work within a set of values that reflect and help to maintain certain social systems which the historian Paul Veyne called matrices (1986). These matrices were both governed by and responsible for historical events. Early European maps of America depicted a land populated by exotic animals and mythological beings; European maps and reports about the New World were permeated by mythological imagery, particularly Christian imagery, in the hope that in this new land, the biblical Eden would be found (Holanda, 2000). Maps and reports were not simply a form of depicting the unknown, of describing what explorers have observed, but they were also used to influence how new lands were perceived and which values they represented to European culture, especially during the sixteenth century and the flourishing Atlantic navigations.

Such matrices are closely tied to Edward Hall's (1969) work on how cultural filters refine the stimuli from the world and determine which will be excluded or absorbed, constantly yet unconsciously determining and

64 *The enactment of space, place and territory*

organizing our relationship with the world. These matrices also influence how space, place and territory are perceived and understood.

Historical matrices explain why space, place and territory get more or less attention in different periods as conceptual tools for explaining social phenomena. Recently, the concept of place has been used as a spear against the abstraction of modernity, which would have privileged space as an overarching concept. Indeed, theoretical and empirical studies on place 'invariably derive from a certain kind of advocacy' (Brockelman, 2003: 36). Territory has become particularly relevant in discussions of globalization, predominantly financial aspects with the transformation of the 'institutional encasements of (...) the state's territorial jurisdiction' (Sassen, 2000: 374), the redesign of European territories after the collapse of the Soviet Union and the establishment and enlargement of the European Union, the global migrations of workers at both the bottom and the top of the labour market, or the long-lasting conflicts in Palestine.

Although place and territory have space at their core, the relationship between the three concepts is not hierarchical. And although the definition of each of these terms presented here singles out their particularities, they are not mutually exclusive. Indeed, space, place and territory are mutually formative, and the similarities and differences between them refine the definition of the others. Space, place and territory exist simultaneously whenever we experience spatial phenomena in different contexts, scales and historical periods. They work in combination – and like Veyne's historical matrices, changes in the understanding of one affects the understanding of the others. They perform as spatial matrices.

In this section I explore the relationships that exist between the three terms when they are experienced concurrently within the same phenomenon, relations which can be harmonious or discordant. The intention is to demonstrate the internal values of each while at the same time to discuss how their characteristics are related, but are not the same. Differentiation is important, because if place were inferior to or smaller than space, for example, or if they were almost synonymous (which is found in the literature), all that would result would be an entropic uniformity.

Following a circular structure, I will discuss how relationships between pairs (space/space, space/territory, territory/territory, territory/place, place/place and place/space) frequently coexist, and how these coexistences may shed light on each concept and on the spatial matrices.

Space/Space

We experience the world through different concepts and materialities of space, and different ways of understanding space coexist without being mutually exclusive. To stay with an example I have already mentioned, astronomers simultaneously experience urban and astronomic space. The entities and flows of each are distinct, and are perceived through a variety of sensorial and cultural filters with different purposes. Astronomers study astronomic space, only taking into account the entities and flows that are part of it, purposefully setting aside any other elements that do not fit in this spatial system. Astronomers work together with their peers and share their findings in laboratories that not only are frequently located in urban spaces but also are influenced by spatial determinants of this space, ranging from required technical dimensions to their location within the city, established by land use zoning. In such cases, astronomers live in different non-conflicting spaces at the same time, and negotiate which entities and flows are filtered to comprise each space according to specific purposes.

The coexistence of different spaces might help us to understand how they influence each other; in the case of urban and astronomic spaces, part of the rhythms of everyday urban life are governed by systems we would consider as belonging to astronomic space (such as the movement of the Earth and the stars). For sailors, astronomic entities and flows are part of the spatial matrix they use routinely, also composed of tides, winds, and the position of the stars.

These examples show that we constantly and simultaneously live within different spatial matrices that influence each other beyond our immediate recognition. Different spaces are untangled by our sensorial and cultural filters, and by different purposes we might have while we experience space.

However, different spatial matrices might also bear or trigger conflicting worldviews. European culture was profoundly continental at the time when golden age of European navigation began in the late-fifteenth century. The Mediterranean represented the maritime world, loosely linking Europe with North Africa and the Near East in the eyes of the average citizen. These two forms of spaces (continental and maritime) involved specific forms of political and economic systems, which influenced the circulation of products, people and ideas. The Mediterranean space had also been shaped by technological influences, since shipbuilding took place as a response to specific winds, sea currents and the length of the expected trips (which were also dependent on navigation instruments). Ocean voyages included entities and flows that did not exist in continental or Mediterranean Europe. In the late-fifteenth century, new technological instruments such as dead reckoning, Portolano charts and the magnetic compass, combined with shipbuilding innovations, allowed long-distance navigation to take place without clear skies or landmarks to guide sailors. As John Law states (1993: 120), the Portuguese

66 *The enactment of space, place and territory*

'were able to convert the currents, the winds, and the rest from opponents into allies.'

And when the Europeans arrived in America, they found human groups with different cultures and consequently with other spatial matrices. For the Native Americans, ancestral spirits, forest forces and other elements which were alien to modern Europeans constituted their space – and reciprocally, the Native Americans could not grasp the elements brought by the Europeans which were essential for spatial perception and organization. When two spatial matrices come into conflict, the dominant social group tends to impose its own matrix as a way of controlling mediation between the human beings and entities and flows of that space. The contact between the Europeans and Native Americans resulted in the elimination or decay of entire cultures, including their spatial matrices, either by physically destroying their material spaces (as with the Inca and pre-Inca civilizations in what is now Peru) or by minimizing and admonishing the way natives related with entities and flows (one of the effects of Catholic religious missions).

Space/Territory

Territory is a portion of space in which values tend to be imposed by a dominant group. These values become embedded in entities and flows. They usually come along with behavioural norms emerging from a well-defined centre, and boundaries yield legitimacy to this territory in relation to other territories and those living within it. But as a portion of space, these values must first pass through the sensorial and cultural filters of those who are supposed to be affected by this territory. Returning to ethology, different species can share the same portion of space without entering into conflict in their ecosystem – ants and lions, for instance, even if they share a few common elements. But they are so distant in biological terms that they actually develop and belong to different territories.

Modern international geopolitics has been used to define the coexistence of space and territory in particular ways. The notion of the nation-state is so pervasive in the modern society that its peculiar form of spatial organization of entities and flows influences what is considered space. Native Americans in general were toppled by the notion of national territories, which ultimately was used as an instrument to abolish their territorial organization. And those that did somehow remain united around their values were stifled by the rigid territorial structure imposed on their fragile world. In this geopolitical space, Canada, as a nation-state, is the territory recognized by other territorial units, which are either homologous in territorial terms or are under its influence. The Inuit share

The enactment of space, place and territory   67

the same portion of space with Canada, but only recently have Inuit and other First People's forms of territory been slowly and prudently recognized and incorporated as a legitimate spatial organization, provided that they do not disrupt the hegemonic territorial matrix of the nation-state.

At times, beneath these territorial differences lies a fundamental sensorial and cultural chasm. On a more essential level, people such as the Inuit apprehend and organize their world by including entities and flows that are alien to the cultural group which commands the portion of space in which they live. We could say that the modern territorial matrix, the base of the nation-state, became so forceful that the entire space has been structured upon it. As a result, any action or object in the modern geopolitical world is only accepted if it passes through the political filter of this idea of territory.

On another level, outer space was thought to be formed of entities and flows so different from those comprising the terrestrial world that it could be perceived and studied independently. However, in Yves Lacoste's geopolitical dictionary (1993), outer space is part of the geopolitics of the Cold War space race between the American and Soviet agencies. Contemporary technological exploration of outer space occurs under the aegis of one particular idea of territory that is fundamentally alien to outer space. And yet, modern society has become so dependent on outer space technologies (such as weather and communications satellites) that Earthly life is extremely vulnerable to any disruption of such technologies, with the 'potential weaponization of space' posing a 'serious geostrategic challenge to the international community' (Al-Rodhan, 2012: 3).

These examples on different scales show how the idea of territory might become so strong and embedded in the way we understand the world that it overtakes its core concept, altering our conceptual and perceptual approach to space.

Territory/Territory

Territories might coexist, but particularly in modernity with the all-encompassing idea of nation-state, this coexistence depends on mutually accepted limits and areas of influence.

Homologous territorial units might have particular rules, values and symbols which are not shared with other units, but they still impart the same notion of spatial organization through territorial concepts and methods. North Korea and the United States are antithetical states, but they are homologous territorial units. In the early-twenty-first century, Al-Qaeda spread across the Middle East and Africa with a strategy of scattering its actions over different territorial units, mining them from

68   *The enactment of space, place and territory*

within and controlling large swaths of different countries without claiming to be a nation-state of its own. Stuart Elden (2009: 32) states that Al-Qaeda operates 'both within and against conventional understandings of the relation between sovereignty and territory'. Al-Qaeda's strategy of controlling territory 'without trying to hold it is designed to destabilize the areas, creating multiple chaotic environments', in which it can 'ultimately erect governing structures after its opponents are exhausted' (Moreng, Gartenstein-Ross, 2015). Acting in the same areas, with the same origin as Al-Qaeda, the Islamic State presented a new problem for the world community of nation-states when it declared that it had established the caliphate in 2014, challenging the world on its own ground: territorial organization based on nation-states. Although Al-Qaeda occupies larger areas than the Islamic State, the challenge that the latter presents has put the international community on alert when it claimed the same territorial organization.

In all these cases, a particular form of territory is hegemonic. However, when spatial matrices are completely different, dissimilar territories sometimes coexist on the same terrain. When the Europeans settled in the Americas, the spatial matrices of the native inhabitants were different from those of the Europeans (and even differed among the indigenous inhabitants). Tribes and peoples had their own territories, which were sometimes imprecise (according to European concepts) but existed through zones of influence or mythical demarcations.

Still, the Portuguese and Spanish had already established their respective territorial domains in the Americas in 1494, only 2 years after Columbus reached the Caribbean islands and prior to the arrival of the Portuguese in Brazil. The Treaty of Tordesillas was an arbitrary line drawn between Cape Verde in Africa, which was already under Portuguese rule, and Cuba and Hispaniola, which had been visited by Columbus. According to this treaty, any land west of this line would fall under Spanish domain and any land to the east would belong to the Portuguese. Here, territorial matrices came before the very existence of space.

Indeed, in some cases, decades and even centuries went by between the Treaty of Tordesillas and the actual arrival of Europeans in parts of the 'discovered' lands. During this period, portions of the land were considered different territories by different cultures without any conflict between those conceptions, or struggles for the hegemony of one territory over another. Native Americans and Europeans were simply unaware of the other's existence. Their territories could overlap on the same land because their territorial matrices had not yet come into contact.

Territorial coexistence can also happen when the territorial matrices of the dominant group encompass other forms of territorialization. The

Kurds have been living for centuries in what is mostly the same portion of space, an area they considered their territory. The mountainous geography of the land they occupy partially explains why they have never developed centralized government structures (unlike other people living in plains areas in the Middle East) (Barkey and Fuller, 1998). Although scattered and speaking several dialects, they share common linguistic roots and family ties, contributing to the creation of strong clan and tribal structures. They lived under the Ottoman Empire for many decades, but because of the Ottomans' universalizing concept of territory (Badie 1997), which was not driven by nation-state methods of controlling land, in no way was the territorial attachment of the Kurds affected, although the Kurds were clearly subservient to the Ottoman Empire, paying taxes and providing soldiers.

When the Ottoman Empire was dismantled in the early-twentieth century, Kurdish lands were divided among Iraq, Iran, the Soviet Union and Turkey, whose first leader promised the Kurds autonomous territory if they supported him (which they did). Now a nation-state, Turkey has put aside this promise, immediately giving rise to the 'Kurdish question'. The Kurds are not claiming a *post-facto* territory, as if bargaining to get a slice of the new nation-state of the Turks. The Kurds are the fourth-largest ethnic group in the Middle East (after the Arabs, Persians and Turks) and only roughly 50 per cent of their population occupies territories in Turkey. The Kurdish territory was always theirs, while the territorial matrix was different, not based on nation-states; when it was altered and accepted as the spatial order by the world's geopolitical powers, the struggle began between two concepts of territory, two forms of inscribing peoples' values and rules upon a portion of space.

Edgar Morin (1969) considers wars of nationality as the dark theme of the twentieth century. But to understand wars based on claimed national autonomy, it is important to consider that several are based not on disputes between previously existing territorial entities, but instead between different territorial matrices. Changes in the predominant territorial matrix caused certain territories previously based on blood, culture or land to be converted (or not) into the new territorial units accepted on the global geopolitical scene. Indeed, international hegemonic states and former colonizers rarely took family ties, clan structures, religion or culture into serious consideration when creating the modern nation-states.

Due to the hegemonic territorial geopolitical matrix, during the twentieth century and early-twenty-first century, only wars between nation-states were considered on the international scene; other conflicts were seen as internal domestic affairs and excluded from global forums. In this regard, the international community tends to see such

70   *The enactment of space, place and territory*

conflicts as a threat to the central power of the legitimate nation-state, seldom organizing international interventions even when these national governments alienate their own people or crushes other internal cultural groups.

A clash of different territorial matrices occurs between Western (originally European) culture and Islamic culture. In modern times, the former is based on the nation-state and any territorial claim is accepted if made within this matrix. Islamic culture, on the other hand, is based on the concept of *ummah*, the entire community bound together by religious principles, which originated when the prophet Muhammad and his companions established their community in the Yathrib (later, Medina) in 622 (Esposito, 1984). The idea of *ummah* guides the whole culture, including space. As Oliver Roy (2004) writes in the introduction to his book, *ummah* is pursued equally by those who distance themselves from enclosed Muslim communities in order to live in a truly universal community of Muslims, and by those who want to achieve an actual *ummah* through political action, and within this group, a neofundamentalist minority concerned with trying to impose Islamic norms.

The conflict between different territorial matrices has emerged cyclically throughout history on different scales. The ideological conflict that marked the Cold War between the communists (led by the Soviet Union) and the capitalists (led by the United States) nevertheless had a common territorial matrix, which disregarded or crushed any other form of territory. As Samuel Huntington (1993: 25) points out, after the collapse of bipolarism, conflicts would occur 'along cultural fault lines' separating civilizations, which are 'defined as the highest cultural grouping of people and the broadest level of cultural identity' (24). Due to the ideological disputes of the twentieth century, civilizations were in some cases dormant, but by the end of this century they were the underpinnings of commercial treaties and military alliances. In this context, Huntington foresaw the re-emergence of a millennial conflict between Western and Islamic civilizations, which would show its force in the early-twenty-first century.

Finally, there are clashes of territorial concepts when they transform themselves from within. In this case, it is not a contrast between two conceptions of territory, with the resulting dominance of one and the foreseeable elimination of the other. Instead, it occurs through changes in the territorial matrices inside a particular world. The emergence of the idea of territories as nation-states, which causes conflict in a Europe which is territorially structured into city-states, feudal societies, principalities and empires, is a clear example of this type of conflict between territories, in which the former still serves as the basis for the next, but is ultimately replaced by it. These profound changes are often triggered

The enactment of space, place and territory 71

by technological, scientific, economic, cultural or political transformations – and frequently involve a combination of these, as in the case of oceanic navigation in the sixteenth century, which was largely funded by Spain and Portugal and gave these countries a territorial dominance reaching far beyond what they could have attained within continental territorial matrices. The transformation in territorial matrices comes through implosion, which sometimes triggers more profound transformations in how we apprehend and understand space. Also, as in the case of oceanic navigation, this might bring about understanding of spatial entities and flows which were not conceivable within the previous territorial matrices.

Territory/Place

Places are portions of space embedded with personal or group values. Places have affective significance to these persons or groups. Persons or groups that do not share the same values might not consider a same portion of space as their places, even if both groups share it. Obviously they are located in space, but places are more than location: their enactment depends on their affective or symbolic appropriation. Catholic churches are laden with meanings only for certain groups, who make such portions of space into their places. For the early Christians, the gathering of two or more people in the name of God made a church, and they used to pray along with Jews and in private homes. Slowly the Christian church developed an architectural semiology fulfilled with spatial (light, scents, forms) and territorial (altar, atrium, nave) elements, which are seen by Christians as their place, because these elements reflect their religious values.

Marc Augé (2010: 853) identifies three spatial characteristics of European sacred space: it is related to temporal events, it is 'planetary', revolving around sacred cities such as Jerusalem, Rome or Mecca, and its architecture is highly codified, with most symbols related to spiritual ascension. Thus, depending on the point of view, a church is a place (for believers) with a powerful territorial semiology (events organizing the actions of believers; which holy place guides its emplacement; where the believer sits or stands is clearly tied to her or his position during the service). Still, for anyone who does not share these values, a church is simply a building, like any other.

Similarly, students and teachers may develop a special attachment to a school. For them, the building is impregnated with affective values, while industrialists or bankers may simply recognize the specific functions of the structure (though they have also attended school). However, from the rooms whose access are permitted for some and forbidden to others

72 *The enactment of space, place and territory*

to the configuration of the classroom, inside the school building there are neatly codified territories. This overlapping of place and territory happens into smaller livable spaces as well. Home as a whole is identified as a place by a family, while in its interior some territories are clearly or tacitly demarcated and respected by family members, territories that encompass the spatial and temporal behaviours of family members. At the dining table, parents might always occupy the same spot, for example, which might have territorial meanings – a father occupying the head of the table still is quite common in paternalistic societies. Only a few minutes after dinner, children doing homework might use the same position without any special meaning. In a more critical approach, Lisa Lau (2006) analyzed the territorialities of women in multiple-family South Asian houses, based on women's fictional literature. Lau (2006: 1100) shows that women are often portrayed as a family possession in massively patriarchal societies, and discusses how women's role is reflected and shaped by 'the landscape of their living quarters'. In one example, based on a novel by Rama Mehta, she discusses the courtyards of a haveli. The haveli (a traditional mansion in the Indian subcontinent) in the book has three courtyards: one for men, another for women and a third, a few steps below, for the servants. This structure clearly defines the position of each group within the household while also highlighting hierarchical negoti-ations: there are passageways between the courtyards, and the men control transit between them, and even husbands and wives are limited by very strict times and locations for meeting.

In spite of the stricture of the territorial meanings which a place might have internally, these connotations do not mean anything to those who are strangers to it. Outsiders simply do not belong to the place, and therefore are not able to recognize its territorial signs. This might be the case with religious buildings. Catholic churches were used as an example of identity places for the faithful; the internal arrangement of altars, niches, crucifixes and confessionals, together with the rituals of the mass and the position of the priest in relation to the congregation, determine the territories and the attitudes expected from all those who accept them. A non-believer can also see the church as a place, but mainly as a place of the other – she or he might recognize signs of cultural identity, but as those of the other, not his or her own identity. Additionally, even recognizing the internal territorial demarcations of the church, this person may not necessarily obey them. Umbanda is a syncretic Afro-Brazilian religion that is mostly found in the northeast region of the country (particularly, the state of Bahia). Although its imagery is pervasive throughout the country and in Brazilian literature, as a non-believer I can recognize only a small fraction of the signs believers see as part of their identity. When visiting *terreiros* (places where rituals are performed)

The enactment of space, place and territory 73

in Salvador, I was incapable of even grasping the entities and flows believers dealt with during the rituals. I was inside a portion of space and could not decode its composition. This portion of space was an identity place for my hosts, and had clear (to them) territorial signs I could barely notice. Writing about his experience with *voudoun* religion in Haiti, Wade Davis (2001: 119) notes that 'cultural beliefs really do generate different realities, separate and utterly distinct from the one into which I have been born.'

A latent conflict between place and territory can emerge from changes in scale. As we have been discussing, the relationship between space, place and territory is not of orders of magnitude (bigger and smaller, more rigid or flexible). Territories and places are portions of space, and a portion can be the whole: 100 per cent and 10 per cent are both portions. Therefore, places can vary considerably in scale, ranging from an aunt's preferred chair for watching her favourite TV drama to regions that particular cultural groups consider as part of their identity. Within the United States, Texans and Vermonters consider their respective identities quite differently; this is partially shaped by their geographical locations (weather, accent, clothing) and their history (The Spaniards settles the former, and the French established the latter in the seventeenth century. Vermont was the fourteenth colony to join the Union, in 1791, while Texas had a more turbulent history of periods of independence before joining the United States in the nineteenth century). Yet when they cross the border to Mexico or Canada, both Texans and Vermonters identify themselves (and certainly be identified) as Americans.

Some places can at times achieve a considerable scale, not just in terms of geographical extent or number of people, but also in terms of meaning. When the signs of a place's identity become strong to the point of dictating social rules, this identity might clash with the territory in which this and other different cultural groups live. The history of Jews, Christians and Muslims in Palestine is an example of places (portions of space embedded with cultural values) where territorial notions of a group's attachment to and rights over a portion of space overlap. Accepting the strong values attached to a place (your own values or those of other people) and having to obey such values is the nebulous and tenuous boundary between place and territory.

This conflict leads to two consequences: on one hand, occasionally social groups try to turn a place into a territory in order to legitimize themselves to other social groups, converting their values into rules and symbols, while on the other hand, dominant groups try to soften their rules and symbols, converting them into values to display a territory as if it were a place. Both cases show a continuous cycle between varied forms of affective and symbolic appropriation of portions of space.

Place/Place

The hundreds of townhouses in Clapham, outside London, all look alike. And yet a particular family considers only one of these houses to be a place they call home. All the others, the neighbours' houses, which may be identical to their own home, are not a place to them – or, more precisely, these buildings are not *their* place. Likewise, believers identify particular temples in the city as theirs, but not other temples of the same religion. Attachments to a place are created through previously existing signs or are juxtaposed to a portion of space, but they are also created through habits and non-visual signs. Residents might identify their own homes among the hundreds of townhouses based on the times they have walked past them after getting off the bus – a synaesthetic way of perceiving space driving what persons perceive as their place.

What someone considers a place also varies throughout time. Street festivals bring a particular identity to a portion of space that vanishes on any other day of the year. During Carnival in several cities around the world, the main streets are transformed. People behave differently; revelers appropriate a portion of space and assume a persona they do not externalize on any other occasion. For these days, the main street is theirs – in Brazil, Carnival revelers even have a king, called *momo*, who receives the key of the city. When Ash Wednesday comes and Carnival is over, this place vanishes. Carnival, as an event, is what makes a place out of this portion of space that otherwise, and on any other day, might not be noticed at all by the revelers.

Although affective identities are related to the concept of place, the co-existence of places can be confrontational. Children fight over the choice of a bedroom, and when they share one, each considers it his or her own: what to include and how to arrange their belongings in the bedroom is part of the construction of their identities through the subjective occupation of a portion of space. Such conflicts can be more extensive and aggressive, as they are between populations who fight for a place both believe to be sacred. Jerusalem is sacred to Muslims, Jews and Christians. For historical reasons, Christians moved the centre of their religious territory to Rome, while the occupation of Jerusalem as their own place and culture is a point of honour and conflict between Palestinians and Jews. Muhammad and his followers first faced towards Jerusalem to pray (this later was changed to Mecca), and the Dome of the Rock is where Muhammad supposedly ascended to heaven. Jerusalem became the capital of Judaism when King Solomon built his temple there in the tenth century BCE. As we have discussed earlier, one outcome of the confrontation between places is that the strongest one rules over all the others, converting a place into a territory.

Space/Place

The cycle closes with place in relation to space. As a portion of space characterized by affection and values, one would not expect conflicts between space and place. On the other hand, places may be used as metonyms for understanding the general spatial matrix in which they exist. Gaston Bachelard (1989) masterfully analyzed the everyday places of domestic settings to study the depth and breadth of the phenomenology of space.

Places are constituted of different entities and flows according to the purpose of the experience. The same person or group, living in the same portion of space, apprehends these elements differently depending on its own activity. This is the case with religious or mystical places. Followers of Umbanda, for instance, do not take into account all the entities and flows which are essential for the constitution of their sacred places when they are living their daily lives. On the other hand, *terreiros* operate as the 'creative epicentre of a web of symbolic, ethnic, social and economic relationships' (Contins, 2014: 252), and Umbanda believers incorporate some religious elements into their daily life, which differentiates their relationship with the urban space that they share with non-believers. And the distance of what constitutes place and space is even wider when we compare believers and non-believers. As Marcia Contins reports (2014: 251), her fieldwork with Umbanda *terreiros* on the periphery of Rio de Janeiro 'made a significant impression on the researchers since all the interpretations we developed subsequently only seemed to diminish and simplify the reality lived by these people.'

The above discussion on the relationships between space, place and territory does not define subcategories, or encompass all possible forms of relationships.

In Lars von Trier's (2003) film *Dogville*, the character Grace is on the run from the mob and arrives in a small town at the end of the road. There is nothing beyond the town. In fact, there is not much in the town either. Dogville is depicted as a theater-like stage, with a few streets and houses drawn in chalk on the ground. There are no doors, no walls and no roofs, only a few pieces of furniture and the bell tower. Still, people knock on invisible doors, open and close invisible windows. They create space through their actions. Grace's first impression is of a 'beautiful little town in the midst of magnificent mountains, a place where people have hopes and dreams.' In order to be allowed to stay in the city, initially for 2 weeks, she has to work for each family. Slowly she creates affective ties with the people, and gradually she feels Dogville is her place. But when the citizens learn she is a fugitive, they demand more free work and start to impose harsh punishment on the outsider. Dogville becomes a hostile territory,

76 *The enactment of space, place and territory*

where ingrained habits and unspoken rules crush Grace, and indeed, all the citizens – who themselves simultaneously experience Dogville as a place and a territory.

One single portion of space can be apprehended by one person through its sensorial characteristics without giving precise meanings, while for another person this portion of space can be cherished as his or her place, and for a third person, it might be impregnated with territorial signs that oversee this person's actions.

The relationships between space, place and territory are context-based and history-dependent. The aim of this chapter has been to clarify that space, place and territory are not defined through hierarchical relations, are not defined through a variation in scale, that one concept is not an extension or reduction of another, and that they also cannot be seen as completely unrelated categories of analysis. They form a matrix in which one term coexists and affects another. The dynamic encounters between space, territory and place are based on their own characteristics, which are reinforced and smoothed through the relationships that are established between them.

References

Al-Rodhan, Nayef (2012) *Meta-geopolitics of outer space*. London: Palgrave Macmillan.

Augé, Marc (2010) Espaces et sacralité. *Cahiers d'Études Africaines*, 50(198/200): 853–856.

Barkey, Henri; Fuller, Graham (1998) *Turkey's Kurdish question*. Laham, MD: Rowan & Littlefield.

Brockelman, Thomas (2003) Lost in place? On the virtues and vices of Edward Casey's anti-modernism. *Humanitas*, 16(1): 36–55.

Contins, Marcia (2014) The city and African-Brazilian religions. *Vibrant*, 11(2): 247–267.

Davis, Wade (2001) *Light at the edge of the world*. Vancouver: Douglas & McIntyre.

Esposito, John (1984) *Islam and politics*. Syracuse, NY: Syracuse University Press.

Huntington, Samuel (1993) The clash of civilizations? *Foreign Affairs*, 72(3): 22–49.

Lau, Lisa (2006) Emotional and domestic territories: The positionality of women as reflected in the landscape of the home in contemporary South Asian women's writings. *Modern Asian Studies* 40(4): 1097–1116.

Law, John (1993) "Technology and heterogeneous engineering: The case of Portuguese expansion". In: Bijker, Wiebe; Hughes, Thomas; Pinch, Trevor (eds) *The social construction of technological systems*. Cambridge, MA: MIT Press, 111–134.

Moreng, Bridget; Gartenstein-Ross, Daveed (2015). "Al Qaeda is beating the Islamic State". *Politico Magazine*, April 14. At: http://www.politico.com/magazine/story/2015/04/al-qaeda-is-beating-the-islamic-state-116954#ixzz3xY3HqHJS

Roy, Olivier (2004) *Globalized Islam: The search for a new Ummah*. New York, NY: Columbia University Press.

Sassen, Saskia (2000) Territory and territoriality in the global economy. *International Sociology* 15(2): 372–393.

Trier, Lars von (2003) *Dogville* [Film].

4 Sensing the city

Space is simultaneously the most abstract and the most visceral of the spatial concepts. Place and territory are portions of space to which we attribute values, with the former leaning towards purely affective values, and the latter aiming at control of the actions and objects under its influence. Space, the conceptual substratum of place and territory, is formed by the relationships between entities and flows screened through sensorial and cultural filters. These sensorial and cultural filters are not immune to historical contexts; therefore, understanding how people perceive space illuminates not only what space means in a particular context, but also how these sensorial and cultural filters are formed.

How cultural filters influence social behaviours and the relations people establish with space have been an underlying question in the works of several scholars. Edward Hall's and Yi-Fu Tuan's books have been particularly relevant in previous chapters, when I proposed the conceptual construction of space. However, since space is the most visceral of the spatial concepts, in this chapter I focus on how scientists and artists explore the way in which people sense space, and how the sensorial understanding of space can send feedback to the space itself, reshaping it and reshaping how other people sense it.

First, I discuss one of the sensorial qualities of space that has lost primacy in modern cities: smell. True, perception varies from person to person. But among the five traditional senses (sight, hearing, smell, touch and taste), smell is the most fleeting. Sight and hearing are highly codified, in general terms as well as in the urban context. Moreover, languages we use daily combine both. Touch, taste and smell are less codified, and permit a more open exploration of the sensorial aspects of space. Here I focus on smell, which has not been codified, and is arguably the sense that yields involuntary memories of portions of space. Additionally, since in this book I am mostly interested in spatial experiences within urban contexts, I argue that smell is the most collectively experienced and shared among these three senses.

80 *Sensing the city*

Second, I explore the use of technologies to understand how we decode space in our brains. Until recently, deep understanding of personal spatial experiences had to be mediated through languages interposed between space and the person. This means that in order to understand how subjects perceived space, a researcher had to rely on oral or written reports or pictorial representations with different degrees of accuracy and subjectivity. These methods have yielded important insights on the understanding of spatial perception and emotional engagements. However, they usually had two caveats: they were based on post-experience reports, and were dependent on the skills each person had with the form of representation used to investigate the spatial experience. More recently, the use of new portable devices, such as electroencephalography (EEG), has allowed researchers to explore brain activity in real time to understand how people experience space.

In both cases, my interest lies not only in how space is sensed. What I highlight in these essays is that researchers and artists have been going a step further and using this knowledge to act upon space, creating spatial interventions that engage people in rethinking how they perceive space and how they give meaning to space, de-automating their spatial experiences.

Finally, I explore the darkness. While in discussing smell and the use of brain activity to create spatial experiences, I am interested in the sensorial filters, and how they select and arrange entities and flows in space, I discuss darkness for its cultural manifestation. In order to do this, I explore how the night has been shifting meanings and how these cultural changes interfere in our perception of space.

Smelling space, smell-space

Smell is arguably the most elusive of the human senses. Most of us cannot intentionally recall a scent. Nonetheless, when a particular odour reaches the nose we are immediately and involuntarily drawn to a person, a situation or a portion of space tied to this odour. Sometimes a full environment comes to mind, and is fully remembered through a single and unexpected sniff.

While smell is not codified, human olfactory memory plays an important role in identifying and making sense of odours. In a study that asked approximately 200 older adult participants to recall memories triggered by words, pictures and smells, Maria Larsson and Johan Willander (2009) showed that olfactory memories are clustered in the first decade of life, demonstrating how smell is deeply ingrained in the early stages of our constitution as individuals. And yet, the profound and ancient memories smells trigger are not paired with our ability to characterize each smell in particular. In an experiment conducted by Dennis Waskul and Philip Vannini (2008) based on people's descriptions of odours, what stands out is the lack of an appropriate and detailed vocabulary to describe olfactory qualities. This does not imply that humans are primordially unable to accurately sense odours or make sense of them, though. In laboratory tests, scientists found that instead of the approximately 10,000 odours that humans supposedly were able to distinguish, our olfactory system can potentially discriminate up to 1 trillion smells comprising a combination of 128 odorants (Williams, 2014). Although this result is purely a statistical possibility, and scientists do not claim that there are 1 trillion discrete scents a person could identify, the point is that physiologically, the human olfactory system is more powerful than was imagined previously. Different from visual objects, which are neatly defined, smells are formed by a volatile and endless combination of molecules. Rather than clearly defined entities, smells are 'experiences of intensities, more like pain or joy' (Rodaway, 1994: 65).

While other species use scents as cues to navigate space, perceive dangerous situations (such as predators) and find appropriate mates, we humans do not use smell with such acuity. Some professionals like sommeliers develop their olfactory skills and can recall the bouquet smelled in a wine they drank in the past, but most of us cannot consciously induce the recollection of specific odours. Thinking of a melody or a painting easily calls them to mind, and we can even reproduce them. But we are unlikely to be able to do the same with the scent of a particular flower. On the other hand, unexpected odours commonly lead to involuntary remembrances of foods and beverage, of people and places. Nevertheless, once such situations are recalled, we cannot recreate an olfactory remembrance of others odours that were also present in this particular situation. Smell can be a trigger of memory, but it cannot be used as a building block of a complex smellscape.

As with any other sense, smell is socially constructed, since odours bear meanings that vary throughout history and among cultures. By that I mean that the social aspect of smell arguably goes deeper than other senses: comprising volatile chemical compounds, odours are hard to block, making smell a fundamentally shared sense – even though the meanings attributed to odours might vary from person to person, and certainly vary from culture to culture. Yet, once a strong scent is present, one cannot turn to another direction to avoid it: smell permeates social space.

As a social sense, odours are part of the urban landscape. In *The Perfume*, the novel by Milorad Pavić mentioned previously, a boy with an exceptionally acute sense of smell describes the eighteenth-century

82 Sensing the city

Parisian landscape in minute detail. Despite the literary qualities of the book, part of its success is based on olfactory stereotypes: 'the maniac sniffing out his prey; the fragrant, hapless maiden; the dangerous savagery inherent in the sense of smell' (Classen *et al.*, 1994: 4).

In the literature on smell, it is quite common to find that odours have been gradually eliminated over the last few centuries. Modernization has brought with it an aversion to odours, along with a normative appreciation of particular scents; variety, improbability and surprise are less important than the correct scent which is expected to match specific portions of space. The de-odourification of the world has created what Drobnick (2006) calls odour-phobia.

Mixed land uses were a common feature in premodern cities. Tanneries, slaughterhouses and laundries were scattered throughout town, and used noxious and smelly materials and chemicals in their operations. Meat and fish markets were part of street life, and sanitation was a real problem in overcrowded cities. Streets were conduits for all types of urban refuse: food scraps, animal and human waste. As late as the early-twentieth century, New York had severe problems related to the stench of nearby slaughterhouses and barns. And when the horses used for transportation and freight died on the job, their corpses were often abandoned on the streets by their owners; it was too expensive to rent or bring two more horses to pull one corpse off of the road.

Nevertheless, Neville Morley (2014) raises the point that a deodorized modern world and its opposite, a smelly past that would be either more rich in an olfactory sense or simply stinkier, are both myths built upon scarce data. The notion of a smelly past, with ancient Roman streets drowning in filth and stench, for example, are based on reports and paintings from that time, not evidence and data. And contemporary scholarly studies engaged in recounting history through the eyes of the masses rather than the viewpoint of the elite have relied more on vivid fictional works than on scholarly, dry reports. This strategy might help strengthen their arguments by contrasting the aristocratic and clean realms with the filthy streets of poor areas, 'the grime to set against the gleaming marble (. . .) decomposing corpses against the scent of rose petals' (Morley, 2014: 112).

In spite of the de-odourification of the modern world, smells still influence how we perceive space, and the meanings we attribute to different portions of space. Capturing this ephemeral feature of space is at the crux of Sissel Tolaas's work. Tolaas has been collecting urban odours for decades. In her laboratory in Berlin, which is funded by International Flavors & Fragrances Inc., she has archived around 7,000 scents and 2,500 molecules so far, ranging from sweat and ashtrays to money and swamp. Considering that smells are physiologically as well as psychologically perceived, each odour in Tolaas's archive is labelled with its chemical composition, how, where and when it was collected, and a story related to it. Also aware of the language deficiency in describing and naming smells, Tolaas has fashioned a specific language, NASALO, to name each scent.

The use of scents to inform space has gained attention in past decades, with international brands creating specific aromas for their stores and cars, and scents to enhance the singularity of restaurants, bars and hotels – in what Classen, Howes and Synnott (1994: 180) call 'olfactory management'. This olfactory landscape is designed to reinforce a brand, and includes logos, catchy phrases and ambient music. Tolaas has been responsible for some of these brand smells. But as Tolaas puts it on her website, she has a more powerful mission regarding smells: 'I reveal what the industry is trying to cover up, deodorize or camouflage.'[1]

Besides her work as a chemist and wide-ranging field research collecting, cataloguing and synthetically reproducing scents, Tolaas is an artist engaged in establishing communication between people and space through smells. She uses scents not to reinforce an image, but to question stereotypes, and to get users to pay attention to odours and spaces by provoking unexpected reactions. In 2005 she attended a reception at the Brazilian embassy in Berlin, dressed formally but drenched in the odour of a man's sweat (Rochton, 2006). The disconnect between a woman's outfit, the venue and her scent confused and shocked people, and made them aware of the usually unnoticed connections between sensorial perception and cultural expectations.

For her 2003 exhibition at the Fondation Cartier in Paris, Tolaas spent 6 months capturing different odours of the *Rive Gauche* ranging from dog droppings to ashtrays and slaughterhouses to demonstrate the kaleidoscopic landscape of one of the most visited regions of Paris, and which pass unnoticed. In Kansas City, she created an exhibition comprised two parts: an installation at the Grand Arts museum, and six tours through different neighbourhoods. For the tours, visitors were asked to collect odours using scratch-and-sniff cards, take pictures of the locations where the odours were collected, describe the scent, and send the material to Tolaas. These maps, pictures and cards were displayed in the gallery. Brittany Lockard (2013: 247), upon visiting the exhibition, noted: 'The frustration I experienced trying to categorize those odors made me intensely aware of how essential scent is for memory, how directly they are tied.' In Mexico City, Tolaas (2010) visited more than 200 neighbourhoods to collect characteristic smells, and filmed 2,000 residents describing the smell of the city. What is distinctive about the smell of a portion of space is the mix of odours; for example, Havana is a blend of tobacco, bergamot and ylang ylang (Girvin, 2010). Such a

84 *Sensing the city*

complexity of smells, which we can perceive at once, ties odours to particular portions of spaces and not to each component individually.

Although smell touches us with less codified filters than sight or hearing, smells trigger powerful individual memories and collective values. Smell helps us demonstrate flows and entities that build up space and seldom appear in conceptual discussions of space, place or territory. But as I have argued here, this is more the result of modern attempts to eliminate, mask and fake odours than the importance of scents as defining spatial features.

Brain spaces: measuring brain activity in urban environments

Finding one's way through space is a brain activity. All sensorial stimuli are processed in the brain, and apprehending, selecting, combining and making spatial sense of such stimuli happen in the hippocampi. Neurologists have been studying how the brain processes spatial recognition for quite some time. Of particular interest here is the fact that research shows that experiencing rich spaces (with varied relations between multiple entities and flows) molds brain activities.

A study led by Eleanor Maguire (Maguire *et al.*, 2000) compared the volume of hippocampi in London taxi drivers and in control subjects based on structural magnetic resonance imaging (MRI) scans of the brain. They found that the taxi drivers had significantly increased gray-matter volume compared to the control groups. The researchers also found that the length of time the taxi drivers had been driving professionally was positively correlated with the volume of the right posterior hippocampus – the brain region responsible for spatial memory related to navigation in space. In another study, Maguire *et al.* (2006) compared the brains of London taxi drivers with London bus drivers, using structural MRI scans. Bus drivers tend to work the same route for a time, while taxi drivers' trips are shorter but more spatially varied. The researchers found a greater volume of gray matter in the mid-posterior hippocampi of the taxi drivers, who were also better at identifying London's landmarks, whereas the bus drivers had more gray matter in their anterior hippocampi and were better at acquiring new visual-spatial information. Although each of the two groups has expansive experience driving around the city and can outperform the other in specific skills, Maguire *et al.* (2006) also found that gray matter volume increased in the posterior hippocampi and decreased in the anterior hippocampi according to how long the taxi drivers had been driving professionally, although this was not the case in the bus drivers. Finally, the taxi drivers reported that their mental map of London became more complex and integrated the more they drove. In both studies, it was clear that spatial complexity and diverse spatial experiences have strong correlations with our brain activities.

Spatial stimuli are also important for cognitive functions and production of new brain cells. Physical activity and exercise are positively correlated with higher cognitive functions (Brown *et al.*, 2013), and patients undergoing medical treatments which demand long periods of immobility (and who consequently do not have complex spatial experiences during these periods) had less production of brain neurons. Spatial enrichments also bolstered the production of new neurons, and consequently mitigated mental illnesses such as depression and anxiety (Schoenfeld and Cameron, 2015). Researchers have also found that it is not necessarily physical mobility that matters, but instead the brain's processing of spatial information: more complex the space, the more brain activity is required.

Medical studies have been using virtual reality (VR) to stimulate naturalistic interactive behaviours based on spatial qualities while at the same time monitoring brain activity. VR can combine visual, auditory and haptic (tactile) stimuli, as well as provide interactive experiences between the user and the virtual environment, and between users. Medical research has also shown that the physiological responses to spatial stimuli in VR environments are similar to those in real-world situations (Meehan *et al.*, 2002). This has led to successful experiments using VR for patients who endure long periods of hospitalization, such as one involving alleviating pain and anxiety in children undergoing invasive medical procedures (Gershon *et al.*, 2003), and another using short-VR sessions to reduce burn-related pain by diverting patients' attention from the pain and propitiating immersive experiences (Hoffman *et al.*, 2001).

Whereas VR brings spatial experiences to people deprived of outdoor living, portable brain-imaging technologies have been used to understand how the brain processes spatial signals while experiencing actual urban environments. EEG is one example. Portable EEG is not as powerful as other technologies for studying brain activity, but its portability allows researchers to survey subjects in urban environments, gathering real-time data on their brain activities while they are actually experiencing specific situations. The EEG-related research highlighted here focuses less on how the brain processes spatial information and more on how space is experienced through reading brain activities.

EEG records electrical activity along the scalp, measuring voltage fluctuations resulting from ionic current flows within the neurons of the brain. EEG has been widely used in clinical contexts for various diagnostic applications, as well as for neuroscience research. Even if it is sometimes less accurate compared to other brain function study methods, EEG has several advantages that make it more appropriate for research in urban environments: it is portable, it is non-invasive, it has high temporal resolution but low spatial resolution (perhaps a disadvantage for

86 Sensing the city

neuroscientists but not for those interested in emotional changes over time) and it is significantly cheaper than other methods of assessing brain function (Mavros, 2011; Li *et al.*, 2015).

Because the technology is sensitive to the subject's movements and external interference, researchers still tend to prefer controlled environments to achieve results that match scientific standards. For this reason, a mix of immersive techniques has been used. Driving simulators allow researchers to assess the performance of drivers with obstructive sleep apnoea syndrome or microsleep episodes (Boyle *et al.*, 2008), as well as the influence of fatigue on driver behaviour (Lal and Craig, 2002). Roe *et al.* (2013) used portable EEG to record the brain activity of twenty participants while they viewed images of urban and natural landscapes, and found that the latter were more associated with higher levels of meditation, while the former were associated with higher levels of excitement. Similar results have been found by Tae-Koon Kim *et al.* (2010), who used fMRI to measure differential brain activation areas in thirty subjects who had both rural and urban life experiences, while they viewed projected images of rural and urban scenes. Chen-Yen Chang and Ping-Kun Chen (2005) used EEG, among other techniques, to assess how thirty-eight participants differently perceived six different configurations of an office space, with and without indoor vegetation and windows.

Despite the technical complications portable EEG presents when it comes to gathering reliable data in outdoor experiments, some researchers, planners and artists have been taking brains out for a walk. Underlying their work is the idea that first-hand experience with the urban context is necessary to actually understand how the brain processes urban entities and flows. And a few of them are taking a step even farther, proposing ways of interacting with space based on brain signals. These brain signals are transformed into communication tools and primary data to shape spatial forms and urban interactions.

The desire to gather real-time brain activity data from an actual urban experience prompted researchers to separately take twelve students for a 25-minute walk in three distinct zones in the centre of Edinburgh using portable EEG. They first went to a shopping street with low traffic, then they strolled in a green space and finally they went to a busy commercial area with heavy traffic. The results showed more drastic emotional changes between the latter two areas, with an increase in engagement and alertness (Aspinall *et al.*, 2013). Arlene Ducao and David Briggs, in turn, developed a bicycle helmet that serves as a tool for communication with other bicyclists, pedestrians and drivers. Equipped with an EEG headset, the helmet measures the levels of anxiety bicyclists experience during their rides, and translates the anxiety level in real time into a light-emitting diode (LED) display on the helmet ranging from green (relaxed) to red (concentrating/stressed).[2] This data is also displayed on maps of the routes taken by the bicyclists, and has a strong correlation between intense traffic and stress levels, for instance.

Examples from the use of VR to simulate spatial experiences and EEG headsets to understand how space is experienced through mapping brain activity, as well as to communicate our spatial experience in real time with other users of space, are shedding new light on how we process the most sensorial of the spatial concepts.

Sensing the night

What happens to space when the lights go out, and darkness comes?

We are so used to grasping space through vision, and we have been illuminating urban space for such a long time with ever more intensity, that we seldom think of space in the dark. It is well known that visually-impaired people use their other senses with great accuracy in order to perceive space, to move through space and to identify particular portions of space. But for those who see, sensing space in the dark is at once disturbing, challenging and exciting.

When darkness comes suddenly, we first feel disoriented. As we cannot rely on vision, we gradually put our other senses to work, or pay attention to their function. Touch allows us to feel our immediate surroundings through textures and temperature. Our spatial range is reduced, and dimensions are resized, as in the Edgar Allen Poe story *The Pit and the Pendulum*: the main character perceives a large and meandering room that he realizes is much smaller when it is illuminated and he can see it. The privilege of vision is so overwhelming that Fiona Candlin (2006: 145) observes that even important art theorists have explicitly or implicitly commented that 'physical contact has no place in a modern appreciation of art', and have belittled touch in comparison to vision. But Candlin (2006: 150) clarifies that 'Touch is not limited to a static contact between our fingertips and a surface. It involves our muscles and bones and complex somatosensory systems.'

If touch makes us feel our immediate surroundings, hearing is able to make space larger. We can hear sounds from far beyond what our vision reaches. Even in daylight, sounds from unseen sources mark spatial and temporal references, such as bells in church towers or muezzins calling Muslims to prayer. Indeed, 'the sounds of a particular locality, its keynotes, sound signals and soundmarks, can express a community's identity in parallel with local architecture, customs and dress' (Revill, 2013: 235). But most of the time we are not aware of the sounds that define our spatial sensing. Because we have vision as our main sensorial referent, we try to match anything that we feel through our other senses

88 Sensing the city

with what we see. When the lights go out, we first get lost in a cacophonous landscape. Slowly we start to locate events in space based on their sounds.

Since I am an urbanite, sojourns into the wild are thrilling and challenging. Bleak night comes and all senses awake; a constellation of sounds emerges. If in a forest, it begins to expand in multiple directions. From the tiny sounds of ants and beetles, which are not part of my visual experience of the forest, to loud sounds of insects or the wind blowing over tree branches, space increases in depth and in height. During daytime in a dense forest, the canopy is often the ceiling of the visual experience. In the dark, the forest grows and the canopy becomes a universe in itself. Sounds of the rainforest are particularly polyphonic and fascinating. Sounds of different ecosystems underlie the concept of soundscape ecology proposed by Bryan Pijanowski and his colleagues: 'Soundscapes represent the heritage of our planet's acoustic biodiversity, and reflect Earth's natural assemblage of organisms' (Pijanowski *et al.*, 2011: 213).

A more mundane and urban example frequently happens to me when I sleep in different locations. In bed, at night, when all the lights are off, noises create a landscape of sounds. When I first moved into an apartment building, ordinary sounds, such as children crying, neighbours walking in the apartments above and people talking in the neighbouring building a few meters away, gradually created an additional layer of meanings for the space. Slowly I got used to them and I could identify the sounds, know where they came from and at what time they would come. An invisible soundscape emerged and enriched the spatial experience of the apartment. In the urban soundscape, passing trains or ambulances, even when they go unheard during the day (within a noisier soundscape), demarcate time and space during the night. Besides linking specific sounds to their sources and locations in space, contextual information also defines the soundscape. Unexpected sounds might put you on alert or trigger different reactions. Depending on where I am sleeping, my reaction varies according to different sounds I hear in the night. If it is a calm and safe city, unexpected sounds coming from the street during the night may only wake me briefly, and do not bear any additional connotation. But in other less secure cities unexpected sounds put me on alert for a while, until I can match them to their locations and possible meanings.

Pervasiveness of electricity and public illumination made complete darkness absent from cities as well. When lights go out, blackouts disrupt modern life – from millions of dollars lost in the economy to more mundane disruptions, such as lack of elevators in skyscrapers or halt in trains and subways. Blackouts might first be a sign of technological malfunctioning: something went wrong, but will be shortly repaired.

It is also a sign of a deep economic crisis, such as countries which mandate rolling blackouts to save energy – such as Venezuela, an important producer of oil which, due to political reasons, in early 2016 mandated official nationwide blackouts of 4 hours each day. But more recently, blackouts, especially when electricity goes off during the night and cities are submerged in complete darkness, sometimes trigger collective fear. In the United States, the Federal Bureau of Investigation suspicion that terrorists were looking for weak point in the electricity grid increased after the 2001 terrorist attacks. As David Nye (2010: 174) puts, 'A generation ago, the immediate question when the light went out was whether a fuse had blown or lighting had struck. But since September 11, 2001, people caught in any blackout wonder if they are under attack.'

So darkness changes the way we perceive space, as well as the meanings we attribute to space – and it varies according to historical moments and cultural contexts. And night is the realm of darkness. For this reason, night spaces are particularly interesting in the discussion of how we sense and attribute meanings to space. As well as how meanings change our perception of entities and flows. Indeed, we become aware of the richness of our sensorial filters when the desolate night comes.

In medieval Europe, night was intensely lived. In the domestic realm, it was common for people to go to bed when dusk fell, wake up soon after midnight to work, talk, make love, perform domestic tasks and go back to bed again. Night was part of everyday life. When the real and imaginary threats night brought were feared, home became a privileged place for building familial ties during the dark hours, creating intimate relations between family members that went far beyond sexuality. Exploring the geographies of domestic places in the era preceding artificial illumination, Robert Shaw (2014) contends that darkness makes people more open to being affected by other objects and bodies. As we partially lose touch with our daylight sensibilities, we are more open to unexpected connections with others, even within the domestic realm, which might strengthen affective ties or worsen violence.

Night was (and still is) full of symbolism. It represents dangers and pleasures, threats and freedom. In societies prior to artificial illumination, darkness and night had a double religious connotation: on the one hand, it was the time in the Judeo-Christian tradition when devotees were closer to the Godly darkness of primordial creation that led to all that exists, but on the other hand, darkness represented all sorts of devilish behaviours from witchcraft to pagan rituals.

In cenobitic monasteries in early medieval Europe, which resembled village-like communities, the office of nocturns was the most important liturgy and the 'lengthiest formal communal office' (Helms, 2004: 184) performed in unlit churches. This ritual was intended to connect the

90 Sensing the city

monks with the pre-creation darkness described in Genesis. Mary Helms (2004: 179) argues that

> This potential for direct nocturnal linkage between the human and the supernatural is temporarily suspended when day intrudes into the spatial temporal qualities of night to force attention onto immediate surroundings and the seemingly urgent, though short-lived, here-and-now mundanity of ordinary daily activities and cares.

Laymen had a positive relationship with the night and its mysteries as well, and opened their homes to phantoms in order to receive magical powers and good luck (Koslofsky, 2011: 30).

In this same period, however, darkness was the domain of demons, ghouls, witches, ghosts and Satan. Carlo Ginzburg (1983) described the nocturnal rituals of the *benandanti*, 'good witches', who protected children and homes from evil witches and cured the bewitched. In sixteenth and seventeenth-century Europe, demonological works occupied popular imagery, leading common people to initiate persecution of witches. 'Witchcraft was real and threatening' (Koslofsky, 2011: 29). Travelling during the night combined these supernatural perils with more concrete ones, such as bogging down in swamps, losing one's way, or being attacked by animals or bandits, reinforcing a 'pervasive nyctophobia' (Edensor, 2013: 424).

The empire of the night in Europe started declining in the seventeenth century. In 1667, Lille and Paris implemented the first public lighting programs in parts of these cities. In 1700, dozens of cities had public illumination, widely using oil lamps that produced ~0.3 lumens/watt. The flickering and faint illumination reconfigured how space was perceived: entities and flows which had been alien to the nocturnal cityscape were now comprehended and acquired other meanings. Unseen shapes and actions came to light, and nocturnal shadows entered the perceptive realm of the city. Streetlights also created new territories. In the seventeenth century, only doctors, midwives and priests were allowed to go out after dusk in several cities in Europe and North America. And any person walking during the night without a torch presumably had bad intentions, and was using the darkness as a cover for their criminal activities or love liaisons. Linkboys could be hired to carry candles and torches to guide those who ventured into the night.

By the late-nineteenth century, although lighting had not yet fully penetrated the domestic realm, street lighting had already reshaped urban life. It allowed people to use the city after dark; it made streets safer, fostered economic growth and made cities a vibrant place to live in. The distribution system that fed gaslights (2 lumens/watt) was implemented in the nineteenth century and allowed theatres and shops, industries and restaurants to be open after dark. As public lighting became an inherent feature of cities, human response to the night went from avoidance to elimination (Jakle, 2001). David Nasaw (1984: 276) summarizes the lighting of cities in the early-twentieth century: 'It was taken for granted that the city's lights removed much of the danger that had once lurked in the dark.'

Indeed, the contrast between lit and dark areas creates territories within the city. In a broad sense, night tends to produce a gender-demarcated territory, where at night women are forced to avoid portions of space they frequent during the daytime worriless (Valentine, 1989). In many cities around the world, people simply lock themselves inside their houses after dusk, in an informal and self-inflicted curfew. In many countries with pervasive urban violence, the streets are avoided after dark, and numerous studies and public programs have been conducted and implemented to reduce crime through better street illumination.

The elimination of the night, or of the darkness, got a new stimulus in the late-nineteenth century and early-twentieth century. In 1879, Charles Brush tested his carbon-arc light (~5 lumens/watt) in Cleveland, Ohio, and witnesses said it turned the night into day (Pursell, 1995). But the event that changed the American nightscape for good happened in 1928, when Thomas Edison switched on incandescent lights (~16 lumens/watt) on the 271 ornamental concrete poles in Bellingham, Washington which comprised a complete illumination system. 'Cities evolved from dark places with only a few flames to guide citizens at night to 24-hour environments under a permanent sun' (Seitinger, 2010). From this point on, modern society has nurtured an 'unquenchable thirst for more light' (Holden, 1992: 56).

Artificial lighting had become so prevalent that it was reshaping not only the urban experience, but also urban form and the meaning of architecture. Robert Venturi, Denise Scott-Brown and Steven Izenour (1977) showed how signs made of artificial lights, and buildings fully encapsulated with them, defined a vibrant nocturnal landscape in Las Vegas, which was rather unexpressive by day. Meanwhile, inside the casinos, 'Time is limitless, because the light of noon and midnight are exactly the same. Space is limitless, because the artificial light obscures rather than defines its boundaries' (Venturi et al., 1977: 49). While Times Square in New York started to use neon lights in the 1930s in advertising signs and to emphasize the features of buildings, in the 1950s Las Vegas would go even further, 'turning the signs into the architecture itself' (Hess, 1993: 22). Buildings without any particular architecture feature, mere warehoused, dressed up in vibrant lights recreated the urban experience and became an attraction in itself.

92 *Sensing the city*

Light festivals around the world celebrate the magic of lights, not by simply turning night into day, but by actually propitiating a nocturnal experience with promises of surprises, excitement and entertainment that only light could bring to cities. Times Square, for example, still represents the acme of the urban lighting epiphany – literally, 'an illuminating discovery', according to the Merriam-Webster dictionary. An epiphany so overwhelming, an urban attraction so powerful, that Times Square buildings and billboards are drenched with light even during the day. The Theater District, where Times Square is located, consumes at its peak 161 megawatts – enough to power 161,000 average houses in the United States.

Nevertheless, it is perhaps a counterintuitive epiphany: have we gone too far in lighting the cities? For purely budgetary reasons, cities are reducing public lighting programs. Considering streetlights alone, a conservative estimate points out that 30 per cent of outdoor lighting is wasted, for it shines directly up towards the sky, where it is of no use for people's activities (Kardel, 2012). Cities around the world have been replacing their streetlights with LEDs (~70 lumens/watt). Meanwhile, several cities in the United States decided to switch off 30 per cent of their streetlights to save money (Davey, 2011). These measures are part of what Jamie Peck (2012) calls 'austerity urbanism' following the 2008 world economic crisis, with a reduced revenue flow and diminishing state and federal assistance for cities.

But the (over)abundance of light has more profound effects on how we perceive space, and attribute meanings to nocturnal places and territories. The insatiable desire for light has increased to the point that two thirds of the world's population 'live in areas where the night sky is above the threshold set for polluted status' (Cinzano *et al.*, 2001). Cinzano *et al.* produced the first World Atlas of the zenith artificial sky brightness at sea level, using models to eliminate the effects of elevation. This atlas was based on data collected over twenty-eight nights and represents the average radiance seen in the set of cloud-free observations. In the United States and European Union, the view of the night sky is so degraded that 90 per cent of the population live as if there were a perennial quarter moon in the sky. Even worse, for 80 per cent of the US population and 75 per cent of the EU population, the sky brightness is close to that of a full-moon sky. Besides degradation of human views of the night sky, ecologists prefer the broad concept of 'ecological light pollution', which includes direct glare, any source of increased illumination and fluctuations in lighting. Ecological light pollution affects ecosystems in different ways, from bird migration and reproductive behaviours to predatory habits (favouring diurnal animals) (Gotthard, 2000). Ecologists also note that light pollution has a stronger impact on the tropics, where species have biological cycles tied to more constant daily cycles, without seasonal differences (Longcore, Rich, 2004). Effects include extending diurnal and crepuscular behaviours for longer hours in animals that forage and hunt under the light, while disorienting organisms accustomed to darker environments. Shortened dark nights also affect the reproductive cycles of amphibians, insects and birds, which in the medium-term will affect the overall ecological balance of entire ecosystems.

If we consider that some of the fastest-growing urban areas are in the tropics, such as those in India, Africa and Latin America, we may expect an increase in light pollution with damaging ecological consequences in the near future. And humans are also affected. In the documentary *The City Dark*, Ian Cheney explores many of the consequences the increasingly glowing night sky has on several species, including humans. Biologists, astronomers and epidemiologists are concerned with the effects that the loss of darkness can have on individual physiologies as well as behavioural and social patterns. Sleep disturbs increase, and doctors pointed to higher incidence of breast cancer in women deprived of sleep hours in complete darkness – mostly those working the night-shift hours. Interviewed for Cheney's film, astronomer Neil deGrasse Tyson stated that the loss of the night might make us lose a 'cosmic perspective'. Myths, social relations and many scientific advances were triggered by the curiosity to find out what was out there in the dark sky teeming with stars. A bright sky would dwarf our understanding and curiosity about what is out there, in and beyond the dark sky.

Dark nights make us use sensorial filters we do not use in daylight, and cumulative values shaping our cultural filters also change how we perceive and attribute value to spaces in the darkness. John Cage's *The Perilous Night* (1944), a composition for prepared piano which was composed at a difficult time in his personal life, brings together minimal monochromes with delicate changes in rhythms and timbres. Listening with our eyes closed, Cage's piece not only makes us more aware of the sounds of the music, of what music could be far from preconceived structures, but challenges our cultural filters through the spatiality it creates: unexpected tones and tempos create new textures in space. Homogenizing space through endless brightness transforms what we perceive as space, and how we create places and territories tied to temporal phenomena.

Exploring space through less-used senses, such as smell, makes us aware of entities and flows that form space but which are not consciously taken into account in our daily experiences. It happens either due to the prevalence of other senses (vision) or to the cultural values attributed to these less used senses(such as with bad and good smells, for instance.

94 *Sensing the city*

Dampening or tampering smells, sometimes attributing moral values to a visceral sense, are creating bland-spaces, which lack diversity and, moreover, distort our sensorial and cultural filters. The use of technologies to directly access how our brain processes the perception and use of space is an attempt to block intermediaries, and to privilege sensorial filters over cultural filters. Researchers are actively working to understand how our brain perceive space using portable devices, what take such experiments out of the laboratories into urban realms. However, understanding that cultural filters are not permanent also helps us to critically assess spatial experiences. Complete darkness impairs our vision and makes us aware of other senses. But this is not only a matter of using different senses when one is cancelled: it is matter of cultural values and symbolisms. Night, which used to be the period of darkness, has been changing values along history. Discussing some of these values and how people perceive darkness permeated by such values, help us to understand that sensorial and cultural filters are intertwined – what makes space even more complex and fascinating.

Notes

1. Sissel Tolaas, at www.researchcatalogue.net/view/?weave=1036
2. http://mindriderhelmet.com

References

Aspinall, Peter; Panos, Mavros; Coyne, Richard; Roe, Jenny (2013) The urban brain: Analysing outdoor physical activity with mobile EEG. *British Journal of Sports Medicine* [Online First]

Barraza Garcia, Roberto; Velazquez Angulo, Gilberto; Romero González, Jaime; Flores Tavizon, Edith. (2014) *LED street lighting as a strategy for climate change mitigation at local government level.* IEEE Global Humanitarian Technology Conference (GHTC), October 10–13.

Bohil, Corey; Alicea, Bradly; Biocca, Frank (2011) Virtual reality in neuroscience research and therapy. *Nature Reviews Neuroscience,* 12: 752–762.

Boyle, Linda; Tippin, Jon; Paul, Amit; Rizzo, Matthew (2008) Driver performance in the moments surrounding a microsleep. *Transportation Research Part F,* 11(2): 126–136.

Brown, Belinda; Peiffer, Jeremiah J; Martins, R (2013) Multiple effects of physical activity on molecular and cognitive signs of brain aging: Can exercise slow neurodegeneration and delay Alzheimer's disease? *Molecular Psychiatry,* 18(8): 864–874.

Candlin, Fiona (2006) The dubious inheritance of touch: Art history and museum access. *Journal of Visual Culture,* 5(2): 137–154.

Chang, Chen-Yen; Ping-Kun, Chen (2005) Human response to window views and indoor plants in the workplace. *HortScience,* 40(5): 1354–1359.

Cheney, Ian (2011) *The city dark* [film]. Argot Films & Bullfrog Films.

Cinzano, Pierantonio; Falchi, Fabio; Elvidge, Christopher D. (2001) The first world atlas of the artificial night sky brightness. *Monthly Notices of the Royal Astronomical Society,* 328(3): 689–707.

Classen, Constance; Howes, David; Synnot, Anthony (1994) *Aroma.* London: Routledge.

Davey, Monica (2011) Darker nights as some cities turn off the lights. *New York Times,* December 29.

Edensor, Tim (2013) The gloomy city: Rethinking the relationship between light and dark. *Urban Studies,* 52(3): 422–438.

Gaston, Kevin; Davies, Thomas; Bennie, Jonathan; Hopkins, John (2012) Reducing the ecological consequences of night-time light pollution: Options and developments. *Journal of Applied Ecology* 49(6): 1256–1266.

Gershon, Jonathan; Zimand, Elana; Lemos, Rosemarie; Rothbaum, Barbara; Hodges, Larry (2003) Use of virtual reality as a distractor for painful procedures in a patient with pediatric cancer: A case study. *CyberPsychology & Behavior,* 6(6): 657–661.

Ginzburg, Carlo (1983) *The night battles: Witchcraft and agrarian cults in the 16th and 17th centuries.* Baltimore, MD: Johns Hopkins University Press.

Girvin, Tim (2010) The Scent of asphalt. Scenting place and the making of fragranced environments. Ca Fleure Bon [blog]. July 10. At: www.cafleurebon.com/the-scent-of-asphalt-scenting-place-and-the-making-of-fragranced-environments

Gotthard, Karl (2000) Increased risk of predation as a cost of high growth rate: An experimental test in a butterfly. *Journal of Animal Ecology,* 69(5):896–902.

Hees, Alan (1993) *Viva Las Vegas: After-hours architecture.* San Francisco, CA: Chronicle Books.

Helms, Mary H. (2004) Before the dawn. Monks and the night in late antiquity and early medieval Europe. *Anthropos,* 99(1): 177–191.

Hoffman, Hunter; Patterson, David; Carrougher, Gretche; Nakamura, Dana; Moore, Merilyn; Garcia-Palacios, Azucena; Furness III, Thomas (2001) The effectiveness of virtual reality pain control with multiple treatments of longer durations: A case study. *International Journal of Human–Computer Interaction,* 13(1): 1–12.

Holden, Alfred. (1992) Lighting the night: Technology, urban life and the evolution of street lighting. *Places,* 8(2): 56–63.

Jakle, John A. (2001) *City lights. Illuminating the American night.* Baltimore, MD: Johns Hopkins University Press.

Kardel, W. Scott (2012) Rethinking how we light at night: Cutting light pollution for more sustainable nights. *Journal of Green Building,* 7(3): 3–15.

Kim, Tae-Hoon; Jeong, Gwnag-Woo; Baek, Hae-Su; Kim, Gwang-Won; Sundaram, Thirunavukkarasu; Kang, Heong-Keun; Lee, Seung-Won; Kim, Hyung-Joon; Song, Jin-Kyu (2010) Human brain activation in response to visual stimulation with rural and urban scenery pictures: A functional magnetic resonance imaging study. *Science of the Total Environment,* 408(12): 2600–2607.

Lal, Saroj; Craig, Ashley (2002). Driver fatigue: Electroencephalography and psychological assessment. *Psychophysiology,* 39(3): 313–321.

Larsson, Maria; Willander, Johan (2009) Autobiographical odor memory. *Annals of the New York Academy of Sciences,* 1170: 318–323.

96 Sensing the city

Li, Zelin; Zhao, Jinhua; Duarte, F; Zhao, Zhan (2015) "My brain at the bus stop: an exploratory framework for applying EEG-based emotion detection techniques in transportation study". In: *Proceedings of the 55th Annual of the Association of Collegiate Schools of Planning Conference*, Houston, Texas, 728–729.

Lockard, Brittany (2013) Sissel Tolaas, smellScape KCK/KCMO. *The Senses and Society*, 8(2): 245–250.

Longcore, Travis; Rich, Cath (2004) Ecological light pollution. *Frontiers in Ecology and the Environment*, 2(4): 191–198.

Maguire, Eleanor; Gadian, David; Johnsrude, Ingrid; Good, Catriona; Ashburner, John; Frackowiak, Richard; Frith, Christopher (2000) Navigation-related structural change in the hippocampi of taxi drivers. *PNAS*, 97(8): 4398–4403.

Maguire, Eleanor; Woolett, Katherine; Spiers, Hugo (2006) London taxi drivers and bus drivers: A structural MRI and neuropsychological analysis. *Hippocampus*, 16: 1091–1101.

Mavros, Panos (2011) *Emotional urbanism.* (Unpublished master's thesis) University of Edinburgh, Edinburgh. At www.panosmavros.com/files/MScThesis_EmotionalUrbanism_Mavros.pdf

Meehan, Michael; Insko, Brent; Whitton, Mary; Brooks, Frederick P. Jr. (2002) Physiological measures of presence in stressful virtual environments. *ACM Transactions on Graphics*, 21(3): 645–652.

Morley, Neville (2014) "Urban smells and roman noses". In: Bradley, Mark (ed) *Smell and the ancient senses*. New York, NY: Routledge.

Nasaw, David (1984) "Cities of lights, landscapes of pleasure." In: Ward, David; Zunz, Olivier (eds) *Landscape of modernity*. New York, NY: Russell Sage Foundation, 273–286.

Nye, David E. (2010) *When the lights went out. A history of blackouts in America.* Cambridge, MA: MIT Press.

Pijanowski, Bryan; Villanueva-Rivera, Luis; Dumyahn, Sarah; Farina, Almo; Krause, Bernie; Napoletano, Brian; Gage, Stuart; Pieretti, Nadia (2011) Soundscape ecology: The science of sound in the landscape. *BioScience*, 61(3): 203–216.

Pursell, Caroll (1995) *The machine in America. A social history of technology.* Baltimore, MA: Johns Hopkins University Press.

Revill, George (2013) "Landscape, music and the cartography of sound". In: Howard, Peter; Thompson, Ian; Waterton, Emma (eds) *The routledge companion to landscape Studies*. London: Routledge, 231–240.

Rochton, Susie (2006) The sweat hog. *The New York Times*, August 27. At www.nytimes.com/2006/08/27/style/tmagazine/t_w_1530_1531_face_smells_.html?pagewanted=all

Rodaway, Paul (1994) *Sensuous geographies. Body, sense and place.* London: Routledge.

Roe, Jeremy; Aspinall, Peter; Mavros, Panagiotis; Coyne, Richard (2013). Engaging the brain: The impact of natural versus urban scenes using novel EEG methods in an experimental setting. *Environmental Sciences*, 1(2): 93–104. DOI: 10.12988/es.2013.3109. At www.m-hikari.com/es/es2013/es1-4-2013/3109.html

Schoenfeld, Timothy; Camero, Heather (2015) Adult neurogenesis and mental illness. *Neuropsychopharmacology Reviews*, 40(1): 113–128.

Seitinger, Susanne (2010) *Liberated pixels: Alternative narratives for lighting future cities – PhD Dissertation*. Cambridge, MA: Massachusetts Institute of Technology.

Shaw, Robert (2014) Controlling darkness: Self, dark and the domestic night. *Cultural Geographies*, 22(4): 585–600.

Tolaas, Sissel (2010) "The city from the perspective of the nose". In: Mostafavi, Mohsen; Doherty, Gareth (eds) *Ecological Urbanism*. Stuttgart: Lars Müller, 146–155.

Valentine, Gil (1989) The geography of women's fear. *Area*, 21(4): 385–390.

Venturi, Robert; Scott-Brown, Denise; Izenour, Steven (1977) *Learning from Las Vegas: the forgotten symbolism of architectural form*. Cambridge, MA: MIT Press.

Waskul, Dennis; Vannini, Philip (2008) Smell, odor, and somatic work: Sense-making and sensory management. *Social Psychology Quarterly*, 71(1): 53–71.

Williams, Sarah (2014) Human nose can detect a trillion smells. *Science Magazine* – News, March 20. At www.sciencemag.org/news/2014/03/human-nose-can-detect-trillion-smells

5 Mapping the city

Every day millions of drivers around the world use interactive digital maps enhanced with global positioning system (GPS) technology. Besides GPS, interactive digital maps exploit an array of onboard sensors and sensors distributed throughout the city that detect and send data about the urban environment to the navigation system of the car, as well as information that the thousands of drivers who share the system input directly – a pothole, a new restaurant, an incident. Interactive maps do not simply display roads, but also traffic, accidents, police stations and a wide range of information that helps drivers find their way around the city (even if they were born in that city). And drivers may choose whether they want the fast, the greener or the calmer way.

Drivers have come to rely so heavily on interactive maps that the most obvious navigational skills, and even basic common sense, are sometimes ignored: if the GPS navigator indicates a specific route, no matter how absurd, sometimes drivers blindly follow it, disregarding features along the way that indicate they might have taken the wrong path. In early 2016, an American tourist in Iceland got his 15 minutes of fame because of the extra R he typed into the GPS navigator of the car he rented after landing at Keflavik airport. The tourist's hotel was on Laugavegur Street, a main road in Reykjavik, Iceland's capital, roughly a 40-minute trip. Instead, the tourist typed Laugarvegur. After 5 hours of driving on icy roads, and disregarding all the signs he passed indicating that Reykjavik was in the opposite direction, the tourist arrived on Laugarvegur Street in Siglufjörður, a small fishing town. In 2009, over-reliance on GPS proved fatal in Death Valley, in California. A mother and her son got lost when the GPS navigator indicated that their fastest route home was a dusty, abandoned mining road. After 5 days trying to find their way out of the desert, in temperatures reaching 49 degrees Celsius, patrols finally found them, but the child did not survive.

If maps are objective representations of the world, why do these situations occur? These cases were caused by either human error

100 *Mapping the city*

(misspelling location names), or a lack of accuracy and updates in the GPS navigators. Nevertheless, both cases reveal over-reliance on a misleading idea: maps are objective and trustworthy representations of reality.

Representations are signs interposed between something (objects, phenomena, actions) and our perception and understanding of that something. Representations, as components of a language, help us to make objects, phenomena and actions understandable to ourselves, as well as help us to communicate particular understandings of such objects, phenomena and actions to others. As representations, maps are impregnated with sensorial and social values. We do not represent what we perceive, but what we are able to perceive. In between something and the representation of this something are the sensorial and cultural filters, which are mediated by language and technology. Ultimately, as the understanding of something is only possible through its representation, sensorial and cultural filters shape what this something connotes: at least (and this is not a minor statement) within each particular historical context. The history of cartography holds plenty of examples of how geographic representations not only reflect how society depicts the world, but also through which values society observes and acts upon the world, and how cartographic representations of the world are used as political tools. Denis Wood and John Fels (1986: 72) discuss two levels of cartographic representation: intrasignification, which consists of 'an array of sign functions indigenous to the map', with which maps can play a role as a 'visual analogue of phenomena, attributes and spatial relations,' and extrasignification, which uses the map as a complete object, and 'trades in values and ambitions; it is politicized'.

Closing the circle of the initial examples that opened this chapter, we could explain the misguided trips resulting from over-reliance on representations based on GPS technologies in this way: GPS navigators have been granted such an aura of trust and objectivity that the representation of the world overcomes the world itself.

In this chapter, I explore mapping as an epistemological tool to understand individual and social relations with the world. The purpose is to discuss cartographic mapping not as a final outcome, but rather as an instrument of inquiry. Maps are not passive representations of reality; consequently, mapping is an active way of investigating the multiple dimensions of space, place and territory. In order to do that, I begin with a conceptual background on mapping as a territorial technology, and discuss how they have been used historically with the purpose to emphasize particular territorial arrangements, and end with examples that have been exploring digital technologies in mapmaking.

Among the spatial concepts discussed here, territory is especially tied to mapmaking. Territory is defined by the control of entities and actions that occur in a portion of space. Territory, understood as a 'political technology', comprising 'techniques for measuring land and controlling terrain', (Elden, 2010: 812) has in maps a powerful tool. Perhaps that is why we 'view the expanding ability of the state – and, to a considerable extent, of private mapping agencies – to map the world and our movements in it with a mixture of awe, admiration, courage and paranoia' (Akerman, 2009). As Geoff King (1996: 16) states, 'map and territory cannot ultimately be separated.' Those with the power to draw and redraw maps define what is considered to be real, what is accepted as being part of reality, as well as the cultural and political values that should mold reality. Maps as a trustworthy representation of reality imply the notion that 'mapped reality appears to be inviolate' (King, 1996: 16).

In many ways, mapping is a form of exercising power over a portion of space. Any mapping implies the selection of spatial features: what to include, and what to leave off the map. Sometimes this process of inclusion and exclusion of spatial features results from particular uses of maps. Ancient Roman maps focused on roads, with scales often measured in time, and contained poor details about (or even completely disregarded) the hinterlands. The political and commercial purposes of these maps were to connect the Roman domains (Elden, 2013). As roads were the backbone of these commercial activities and military movements, Roman maps were centred along the extensive road network.

Sometimes, maps can be seen as a territorial technology, intentionally excluding particular features that aim to reinforce certain worldviews. In the modern era, the most common realm in which mapmaking as a territorial technology is discussed is the institution of nation-states. Nation-states have used maps to buttress portions of space appropriated by conquerors or dominating powers, and used well-defined boundaries to enforce specific rules and behaviours. Chinese maps not only depict Tibet as pertaining to China, but since the emergence of Communist China the 'Geographical Place-Names Committee' has constantly Sinocized Tibetan place names,[1] as if China were taking possession of these territories by renaming them and conveying these names to international media outlets. In contrast are best-selling Chinese nationalist books portraying modern-day China divided into five territories: the People's Republic of China, Tibet, East Turkestan, Inner Mongolia and Manchuria. In this case, the goal is to denounce to Chinese readers the threats that globalization and the Western political influence might represent to the country's territorial sovereignty (Callahan, 2009). Guatemala, in the Caribbean, often displays maps on billboards and

102 *Mapping the city*

passports that feature a dotted border with Belize, or even more aggressively show the latter to still pertain to the former – despite mutual recognition as different countries since 1991.

Mapmaking as a territorial technology has also been translated to the urban scale. Clear-cut limits between cities are rare; there are no checkpoints, no border controls and no patrols controlling flows between most of the cities – with few and radical examples, such as Berlin during the Cold War, or the highly controlled border between Tijuana, in Mexico, and San Diego, in the United States. In most cases, looking at satellite images of large urban regions, we see constructed areas with varied densities. Concentrations of high-density areas sprawl to low density, and isolated buildings pepper the landscape, interconnected by infrastructure such as roads, bridges and electrical transmission lines, all sharing the natural substratum. One example of the natural substratum transformed by urban use is water supply systems, which rely on watersheds that are likely to serve several cities. Large infrastructure, road networks and electricity grids usually do not halt at city limits – and for this reason the exceptions are quite impressive, such as the parallel highways running along the Mexico-United States frontier between Ciudad Juarez and El Paso.

Within cities, it is not uncommon to leave slums off official maps. This is not because of a lack of surveys or aerial imagery capable of mapping the labyrinthine structures of slums, but rather due to a political decision which denies those living in these areas the rights that all other citizens have. As in many other cases around the world, being 'off the map' has dramatic consequences for Kaula Bandar, a 50-year-old slum with roughly 12,000 inhabitants located near the Mumbai stock exchange. As residents of a 'non-notified slum', the inhabitants of Kaula Bandar lack access to the public water supply, sanitation and government-built toilet blocks, solid waste collection and other public services. Consequently, residents pay a high toll in terms of economic opportunities and public health (Subbaraman *et al.*, 2012).

But the point I would like to make here is that one type of territorial approach has been driving urban planning for decades: zoning. Zoning is based on a set of normative and prescriptive rules and ordinances. It divides the terrain into clear enclosures, and regulates which activities can exist within each area, which population and built densities are allowed, which minimum and maximum heights, area and building frontage are permitted, and a set of other less-spatial rules. Zoning is so pervasive that quite often it has replaced design and other forms of planning in shaping space and social interactions. Zoning is authoritative planning, freezing established power relations, and hampering social and spatial rebalancing. Zoning expresses the use of mapping not as an investigative instrument to inquire how portions of space are appropriate (as we will explore further on), but as an instrument to enforce a viewpoint. Once mapped, it is real. With this oxymoronic logic, planning through zoning has been attempting to determine not what the city is, nor how the city could be, but what is the correct city.

Zoning maximizes certainty. In zoning, landowners and developers see an 'incontrovertible brief for the future use of the land and the potential for development', and public officials avoid future decisions to be made 'according to the whim, chance, or political expediency' (Booth, 1995: 104). Although zoning is an instrument for securing private and collective rights upon land, and a balance between regulatory and discretionary systems is possible, the role of zoning in planning practice has acquired mythical powers. Much more than the legal basis upon which the city could be designed and shaped, zoning became a design tool in itself. Zoning is part of the quantification of the urban dynamics, 'figuring out the least-cost alternative to achieving desired goals', where 'subjectivity [is] disguised by numerical exactitude' (Fainstein and DeFilippis, 1996: 7).

This type of territorial planning approach is reinforced through maps that bear almost no relation to the topographical and social features of a portion of space. Likewise, although this approach determines which activities parts of a city may contain, and yields general rules about the form of the container, it does not bear any vision of how the city will look; it is as if physical and social features, the very essence of urban life, were banished from urban planning. Zoning regulations are detailed, but are devoid of urban dynamics, while zoning maps are colourful but soulless. Zoning maps are the epitome of bureaucratic city planning, of a territorial approach to urban life.

The use of maps to underpin social values and to enforce political viewpoints reveals how their 'extrasignification' is wielded. The 'intrasignification' of maps also discloses the power that cartography has over society, since cartographic norms imply the 'correct' way of representing the world. It is as if cartographers create spatial panopticons (Harley, 1989), using the rules of how natural and built landscapes are abstracted, how social phenomena are normalized, and how rhetorical styles are employed to convey the cartographic worldview.

In cities, mapping is much more intriguing when it is employed to inquire how portions of space are appropriated and transformed by individual or social values and uses: how mapping can allow us to unveil, represent and advocate for urban places and spaces.

In the 1950s, Kevin Lynch (1960) used simple diagrams to synthesize how residents of Jersey City, Los Angeles and Boston selected paths and identified borders or landmarks while positioning themselves and finding

104 *Mapping the city*

their way through their cities. Lynch's maps represented a collective and social image of the city that did not necessarily coincide with cartographic maps. Lynch showed the urban structure of each of these cities based on the perceptions of its residents, putting aside metric values, the precise location of objects and overarching mapping techniques. Lynch's works opened up the possibility of adding multiple layers of urban meanings to the city. Since then, researchers have been capturing affective values attributed to portions of space based on the drawings, photographs and personal journals of residents.

At the same time that Lynch was conducting his work, Situationist International developed the idea of psychogeography, which underlies attempts to subvert the power exerted by official cartography, and builds up a collective understanding of the city through its actual use by a variety of people. Situationists denounced the schematic and oppressing characteristics of panoptic cartographies, but did not suppress mapping altogether; rather, they explored the power relations and the possibilities the city presented at street level. Their intent was to understand how subjective feelings and the geography of the urban environment affect and transform each other. Their critical procedure was the *dérive*: a pair or small groups of people wandered through the city exploring new paths, exercising their awareness of varied aspects of urban life during their stroll and thinking of ways to transform the space. *Dérive* 'organize[s] movements metaphorically around psychogeographic hubs' (McDonough, 1994: 64), where time and actual experiences organize entities and flows that compose space. With their critical strolling, the situationists intended to 'transgress the lines of habit without becoming subordinate to the dictates of chance' (Pinder, 1996: 417). Another method was called *détournement*, or diversion, through which the situationists took images and words out of their original context and juxtaposed them somewhere else in order to disrupt their sedimented meanings and open up new possibilities. The most famous map of this approach was *The Naked City*, created in 1957 by Guy Debord, who became an important cultural critic and philosopher.

In 1974, Denis Wood began a decade-long project with his students at North Carolina State University to map Boylan Heights, a neighbourhood in Raleigh. In the beginning, since they were not familiar with the area, they mapped every permanent and transient entity from streets and water mains to the light cast by streetlights on the pavement and the colours of the leaves. On Halloween of 1982, they took pictures of all the carved pumpkins and mapped them, and they mapped every address mentioned in the ninety-six newsletters published by the Boylan Heights Association. 'People who get mentioned in the newsletter carve jack-o'-lanterns and put them on their porches on Halloween' (Wood,

2004: 107). Despite any likely 'freakonomic' conclusion, for Wood this correlation indicated measures of class and tradition, and as the neighbourhood passed through a process of gentrification, 'there are more jack-o'-lanterns everywhere' (*ibid.*)

Becky Cooper distributed an outline map of Manhattan with Broadway and Central Park as the only additional features to hundreds of New Yorkers, along with a single request: map your memories. In the published version of this affective mapping of Manhattan she compiled 75 of these maps. Contributors included poets, painters, journalists, librarians, musicians and an astrophysicist. Some used the base map as a blank sheet for free-hand drawing or writing particular memories; others covered Manhattan with a dense forest, simply put one or several dots marking where one met his wife, another mapped his three lovers and six wives, or shaded parts of the city related to particular emotions such as depression, anxiety, hope and joy. Rather than trying to find common denominators among these maps, Cooper (2013: 9) highlights the subjectivity of each mapmaker as the way of recounting 'an honest story of a place'.

Adding subjective layers to ordinary maps got a boost from social media and maps and satellite images available on the Internet. Tagging photos to particular parts of the city and mapping the most cherished spots of a city based on tweeted messages or social media references is common. Using photos posted on social media, researchers have illustrated how different social groups (e.g., tourists and residents) experience the same city, and by combining the spatial tags with the cyclical or episodic tags of the photo taken in different cities, researchers argue for distinctive 'social timespaces', or visual signatures of each city.

In fact, the rapprochement of subjective and objective spatial features in the mapping of the city has a long history. Before and during the golden period of European oceanic navigation in the sixteenth century, cartographers had to rely on travellers' stories to fill in the blank spaces on the maps pertaining to regions that had not yet been properly surveyed. Sometimes geographic information was added, and sometimes figures and notes were included around the maps with quasi-cartographic elements such as religious and mythical cosmologies. These were slowly set aside in favour of scientific cartographies.

The Renaissance saw the resurgence of the works of Claudius Ptolemy, who lived in Alexandria around 100–170 BCD. At the city scale, Naomi Miller (2003: 27) sees a 'watershed in city mapping' in the Urbino Codex (Vat. Urb. Lat. 5699, from 1469) with the emergence of a more precise cartography based on Ptolemaic principles. The map of Florence (fol. 126v) shows clear limits of the walled city and out-of-limit topographical features, mixing birds-eye views and parallel perspectives. Buildings are

Figure 5.1 Civitas Florentiae, detail of the fresco Madonna della Misericordia, Loggia del Bigallo, Florence, c. 1350. © ASP Firenze Montedomini.

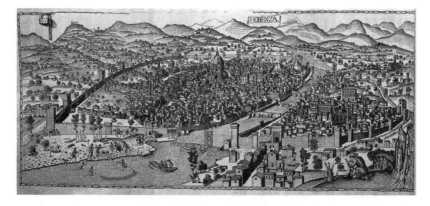

Figure 5.2 Francesco Rosselli, *View of Florence with the Chain*, 1480 © Musei Civici Fiorentini. As stated by Naomi Miller (2003: 129).

Mapping the city   107

located with fair precision, although they are depicted as isolated units and are not linked by any urban infrastructure, with mixed points of view and uncorrelated scales – the houses are almost the same size as the Duomo. Scholars have compared two depictions of Florence, one medieval (*Civitas Florentiae*, detail of the fresco *Madonna della Misericordia*, Logia del Bigallo, Florence, c. 1350) and another from the Renaissance (*Map with a chain*, 1480), pointing out that the dramatic difference between them in just one century is not just the result of the transformations in the city, but rather derives from the technical, artistic and scientific revolution triggered by the invention of linear perspective in the fifteenth century. While in the former depiction the buildings seem to be clustered together, as if the artist and the viewer could walk through the city, have a tactile experience, and explore each building through all its sides (Edgerton, 1975), in the latter depiction the objectivity of linear perspective replaced the body as 'vehicle of knowledge (. . .) [making it] *dispensable*', replacing it with a 'detached eye, a disincarnated eye' (Romanyshyn, 2008: 509). However, as stressed by Samuel Edgerton Jr, an author who is often cited when medieval and Renaissance Florence are compared, the clear separation between a 'decorative phase' and a 'scientific phase', marked by the emergence of modern techniques such as perspective and Ptolemaic cartography with latitudes and longitudes, is misleading. 'Instead, the new grid cartography, especially in the hands of the Roman popes, tended to reinforce faith in the divine mission of Christianity to convert the world. (. . .) become in its own right a talismanic symbol of Christian authority' (Edgerton, 1987: 11).

> Emerging from the medieval frame, the educated citizen of the fifteenth century was confronted with previously unimagined possibilities, many of which are reflected in the city maps of the day. To humanists these maps impart specific knowledge of the world beyond their immediate domains; to statesmen, the potential for future conquests. To merchants they present the existence of expanded opportunities; to travelers, the means to pursue exciting adventures. Even for members of an aristocratic court society the maps serve an important purpose: displaying their wealth and artistic sensibility.

The first modern atlas, the *Novissima Exactissima Orbis Terrarum Descriptio Magna*, published in Antwerp in 1570, combines the precision of the Ptolemaic cartographic system with decorative elements including religious stories (Adam and Eve are depicted at the top of the map), historical scenes, urban views and sea monsters. Whereas modern cartography gradually set aside religious and mythical elements and

108 *Mapping the city*

Figure 5.3 Joannes Vermeer, *The Geographer*, 1668–1669 © Staedel Museum

favoured scientific observation, its social symbolism increased with European conquests of new lands and the establishment of commercial routes to America and Asia. In seven of the thirty-four known paintings by Jan Vermeer, maps are either a key element on the background or are the main theme, such as in *The Astronomer* or *The Geographer*.

Maps were also common in works by other seventeenth-century Dutch painters, such as Johannes Moreelse, Jan Steen, Gerrit Dou and Jacob Ochterveldt. Vermeer is not only the most famous painter among them, but is arguably the one who depicted a higher number actual

Mapping the city 109

maps in this paintings. This highlights the importance of maps as technical, commercial and social artefacts at his time (Welu, 1978). The Netherlands at that time was a major player in international maritime trading, and maps representing 'state power and world dominion (were) combined with progress in science and in arts' (Livieratos and Koussoulakou, 2006: 139). In the Netherlands, as well as in other Renaissance artworks, 'maps represent a visual summa of contemporary knowledge, power and prestige, some of it religious but most of it secular' (Woodward, 1987: 5).

Therefore, although modern cartography has been presented as a technical and scientific method for capturing discrete and continuous features of space which are detached from moral and political stands, the truth is that: first, as a cultural filter, mapmaking depicts a portion of space inasmuch as it carries the moral and political views of the mapmakers, and second, mapmaking has always been influenced by available technologies and scientific knowledge. Cognitive and emotional maps of the city, whether using traditional methods such as drawings, photos and personal journals or social media to map uses of or affection towards certain portions of space, demonstrate how mapping can be used to disclose and reinforce affective appropriations of portions of space – thus mapping places out of portions of urban spaces.

But mapping, which is dependent on scientific and technological advancements, can also change and challenge the common entities and flows we take for granted when defining what urban space is. Indeed, what advanced mapping technologies emphasize anew is not only and not even necessarily more precise mapmaking. Rather, the use of pervasive information and communication technologies might bring with it the possibility of capturing entities and flows we could not perceive previously, and new forms of engaging with space.

A series of personal devices and small sensors allows real-time mapping, or the construction of maps 'through mapping practices, an inscription in a constant state of re-inscription' (Kitchin and Dodge, 2007: 335). An everyday example is the use of real-time mapping tools embedded in mobile devices, such as cell phones with access to GPS technology. They locate the person, match the location with public transportation flows, with traffic and pollution levels, locate friends that happen to be in the same area through social media activity, and then propose routes that have a higher possibility of social interactions or are faster or less polluted, redrawing the map according to a set of parameters chosen by the user. In this case, 'the map emerges through contingent, relational, context-embedded practices to solve relation problems' (Kitchin and Dodge, 2007: 342). Despite the fluidity of this approach to mapping, one that is more attuned with spatial practices,

110 *Mapping the city*

in a sense it seems as if the all-encompassing panoptical cartography is being replaced with an egocentric and ephemeral cartography, one which is unaware of any spatial elements (natural, artificial and social entities and flows) that are not directly related to the user's immediate interests. These elements can be within the user's field of view or physically close, but not related to the user's immediate interest, they are dismissed.

This egocentric mapping, where entities and flows taken into account to create the personal map have to fit into a restrictive taxonomy, leaves little room for spatial exploration, for serendipity. Aware of this, people are proposing to reintegrate surprise and the unexpected into digital mapping.[2] Obviously, at the fast pace of technological developments, these examples are doomed to be outdated soon. But they give an idea of what has been attempted to create new cartographies using the abundance of digital traces we leave when using digital technologies.

In *Invisible Cities*,[3] Christian Marc Schmidt and Liangjie Xia (2011) created maps of New York, San Francisco, Seattle and Tokyo based on real-time social media activity. Every time a tweet or Instagram image is posted, a dot appears at the location where the activity occurred, and high and low densities of data create additional social media topographies over the city map, with peaks and valleys that change throughout the day according to social media activity. All activities are tagged, and selecting one tag forms a content-based network linking all points of the city where the same word has been used. In this example, actions and affective expressions help to map urban space as the dynamic system it is, not as a permanent and immobile basis, as occurs with traditional cartographies.

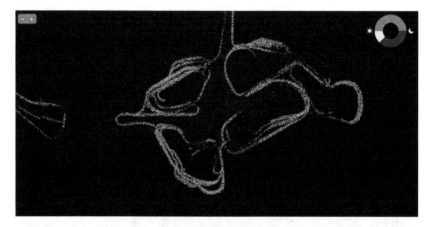

Figure 5.4 Senseable City Lab, *Hubcab*, 2014 © MIT Senseable City Lab

Mapping the city 111

The groundbreaking work that used locative media activity to create a dynamic urban cartography is arguably *Real Time Rome* created by the Senseable City Lab for the Venice Biennale in 2006. The project gathered and interpolated data from cell phone activities as well as real-time location of buses and taxis in Rome (Calabrese and Ratti, 2006). Focusing on the final match of the FIFA World Cup between Italy and France on 9 July 2006, the mapping of cell phone activities during the day showed peaks of social activity when Italy scored, low activity during half-time, and peaks and flows of people during the celebration of Italy's victory. Activities also moved around the city, from residential areas in the morning to regions with bars and restaurants during the match, when supporters gathered to cheer for Italy and then to celebrate at the *Circolo Maximo*. A few years later, in *HubCab*, the SENSEable City Lab mapped the pick-up and drop-off points of around 170 million taxi rides in New York City over the space of one year. The number of points is so dense that the street map of New York emerges, even though the researchers did not use a cartographic map as a baseline. More interestingly, what emerges from this map is a potential shareability network. Using statistical models of the trips taken from each point to each specific destination, the researchers proposed that if any user could delay his or her trip by 5 minutes, virtually all the taxi rides in New York could be shared (Santi *et al.*, 2014). These are examples of how mapping the city in real time, understanding how people use the city through their flows that vary with the occurrence of events rather than relying on static and panoptical maps, might shed light on the very essence of urban space: the relations established between entities and flows.

Maps are entrenched with technological, social, cultural and political values. They have been used mostly as representations of particular worldviews, and to enforce them over a portion of space. In these cases, maps are the outcome of strict, codified language processes and reify particular spatial appropriations. In this chapter, I emphasized mapmaking rather than maps. Mapmaking is an epistemological tool to discuss the construction of space, place and territory. The analysis of mapmaking, which is also entrenched with technological, social, cultural and political values, sheds light on how entities and flows are perceived and organized, as they are filtered by sensorial and cultural filters. In this sense, interest in mapmaking lies not in its outcomes, but rather in how these filters change throughout history due to technological and cultural transformations, and, moreover, how changes in the way people conceive, perceive and appropriate space, place and territory can be analyzed through maps.

112 *Mapping the city*

Notes

1. *Tibet, activism and information.* Blog, at https://tibettruth.com/2011/03/15/national-geographic-wiping-tibet-off-the-map/
2. Poetic Places, created by Sarah Cole and the British Library (at www.poeticplaces.uk) and the app Likeways, created by Martin Traunmueller, Barlett's alumnum (https://itunes.apple.com/us/app/likeways/id1054718491?mt=8) are examples.
3. Invisible Cities project at www.schemadesign.com/work/invisible-cities

References

Akerman, James (2009) "Introduction." In: Akerman, James (ed) *The imperial map*. Chicago, IL: Chicago University Press, 1–10.

Booth, Philip (1995) Zoning or discretionary action: Certainty and responsiveness in implementing planning policy. *Journal of Planning Education and Research,* 14(2): 103–112.

Calabrese, Francesco; Ratti, Carlo (2006) Real time Rome. *Networks and Communication Studies,* 20(3–4): 247–258.

Callahan, William (2009) The cartography of national humiliation and the emergence of China's geobody. *Public Culture,* 21(1): 141–173.

Cooper, Becky (2013) *Mapping Manhattan. A love (and sometimes hate) story in maps by 75 New Yorkers.* New York, NY: Abrams.

Edgerton Jr, Samuel (1987) "From mental matrix to *mappamundi* to Christian empire: the heritage of Ptolemaic cartography in the Renaissance." In: Woodward, David (ed) *Art and cartography: Six historical essays.* Chicago, IL: Chicago University Press, 10–49.

Elden, Stuart (2010) Land, terrain, territory. *Progress in Human Geography,* 24(6):799–817.

Fainstein, Susan; DeFilippis, James (1996) "Introduction: the structure and debates of planning theory." In: Fainstein, S; DeFilippis, J (eds) *Readings in planning theory.* Chichester: Wiley Blackwell.

Harley, John Brian (1989) Deconstructing the map. *Cartographica,* 26(2): 1–20.

Hochman, Nadav; Manovich, Lev (2013) Zooming into an instagram city: Reading the local through social media. *First Monday,* 18(7). At: http://firstmonday.org/ojs/index.php/fm/article/view/4711/3698

King, Geoff (1996) *Mapping reality: An exploration of cultural cartographies.* New York, NY: MacMillan.

Kitchin, Rob; Dodge, Martin (2007) Rethinking maps. *Progress in Human Geography,* 31(3): 331–344.

Livieratos, Evangelos; Koussoulakou, Alexandra (2006) Vermeer's maps: A new digital look in an old master's mirror. *ePerimetron,* 1(2): 138–154.

McDonough, Thomas (1994) Situationist space. *October,* 67: 58–77.

Miller, Naomi (2013) *Mapping the city. The language and culture of cartography in the Renaissance.* London: Continuum.

Romanyshyn, Robert (2008) The despotic eye: an illustration of metabletic phenomenology and its implications. *Janus Head,* 10(2): 505–527.

Pinder, David (1996) Subverting cartography: The situationists and maps of the city. *Environment and Planning A,* 28(3): 405–427.

Santi, Paolo; Resta, Giovanni; Szell, Michael; Sobolevsky, Stanislav; Strogatz, Steven; Ratti, Carlo (2014) Taxi pooling in New York City: A network-based approach to social sharing problems. *PNAS,* 111(37): 13290–13294.

Schmidt, Christian Marc; Xia, Liangjie (2011) *Parsons Journal for Information Mapping,* 3(1): 1–6.

Subbaraman, Ramnath; O'Brien, Jennifer; Shitole, Tejal; Sawant, Kiran; Bloom, David; Patil-Deshmukh, Anita (2012) Off the map: The health and social implications of being a non-notified slum in India. *Environment and Urbanization,* 24(2): 643–663.

Welu, James (1978) The map in Vermeer's "Art of painting". *Imago Mundi,* 30: 9–30.

Wood, Denis; Fels, John (1986) Designs on signs/myth and meaning in maps. *Cartographica,* 23(3): 54–103.

Wood, Denis (2004) "Two maps of boylan heights." In: Harmon, Katharine (ed) *You are here.* New York, NY: Princeton Architectural Press.

Woodward, David (1987) "Introduction." In: Woodward, David (ed.) *Art and cartography. Six historical essays.* Chicago, IL: Chicago University Press, 1–9.

6 Conceiving the city

Brasília: the construction of an idea

Space, place, territory and the transformation of cities

The political and ideological battle between Robert Moses and Jane Jacobs marked the history of twentieth-century New York. Moses entered public office in the 1920s and worked for the city for almost 40 years. During his tenure, he created 658 playgrounds and 17 public swimming pools across all of New York's neighbourhoods, encouraged slum clearance programs, built bridges across the Hudson and many parkways, and was also behind the construction of several important buildings such as Lincoln Center in Manhattan and the World Fair complex in Queens. His faith in highways as instruments of urban renewal had been criticized since the 1930s. But the debate became increasingly acrimonious in the late 1950s, when Jacobs and other civil rights advocates and scholars such as Lewis Mumford criticized Moses for spending huge amounts of money on car-oriented projects and not enough on public transportation, and for reconstruction projects that tore apart traditional neighbourhoods and communities. Moses' reign ended as the public got tired of his long tenure, civil-rights movements emerged, and after two influential books were published: in 1974, Robert Caro's Pulitzer Prize winning *The Power Broker*, which demonized Moses for promoting socially and racially prejudiced projects, and Jane Jacobs's 1961 *The Death and Life of Great American Cities*, which criticized Moses's huge and disruptive modernist projects and advocated a small-scale and community-based approach to urban life. Only recently has a more balanced view of this ideological battle between Moses and Jacobs been permitted in academia, with books and exhibitions showing how Moses reshaped New York, often actually favouring historically disregarded communities, while Jacobs's advocacy for the neighbourhood scale and small businesses has also

116 *Conceiving the city*

been appropriated in gentrified urban projects, using her discourse against her cause.

This well-known example of a dispute between two urban approaches is highlighted here to show that when parts of a city are radically transformed, the very ideas of space, place and territory are also transformed. Briefly, one could say that Moses favoured the spatial transformation of New York, because only by designing for the emerging entities and flows of the modern world could the city thrive, while Jacobs showed that some of these infrastructure projects generated internal territorial boundaries in neighbourhoods that had previously been unified, and that these projects also undermined the communities' sense of place.

Conceptual disputes between different views of space, place and territory occur on different urban scales. They occur in small-scale projects, such as when slum tenements are bulldozed to construct social housing or other urban amenities, often leading to the eviction of families and changes in their daily routines. They also underpin large urban reconstructions, some impacting not only the people who are directly affected but also the entire field of urban design and planning. In the second half of the nineteenth century, expansion plans in Paris (under Georges-Eugène Haussmann) and Barcelona (led by Ildefonso Cerdà) dislodged thousands of people who had been living in the old, labyrinthine central areas of these cities for generations. The razed areas created space for long, broad avenues and boulevards, parks and squares, and sanitation and infrastructure projects. Yet these projects were not just intended to change the physical aspects of these cities, but proposed new forms of planning and living in cities. Modern urbanity implied considering entities and flows typical of the emergence of industrialization, urban bourgeoisie and the technological and scientific approaches to different aspects of social life.

Such nineteenth- and twentieth-century urban reconstructions produced new concepts of urban life, and influenced urban planning and design on different scales. But a more radical approach might arise from the opportunity to design and build a new city from scratch. In this case, all possibilities are open. While time and memory still lurk in every idea put forward in urban reconstruction projects, the hopes and the anguish of the future are the only time dimension underlying the projects for new cities. For new cities conceived within the ordinary urban *zeitgeist*, their existence is only a point on a continuous timeline. They are born from old and ordinary urban concepts, such as the hundreds of new cities built in China after the 1978 Cultural Revolution. Their construction helps understand rapid global urbanization, but lacks any appeal to discuss a global urbanity. They are simply more of the same – in a humongous scale, true, but without shedding any light in alternative contemporary urbanization. On the other end of the spectrum are cities which either coalesce or catalyze ideas of what urbanity could be. These urban ideas bring with them the intention of bending time, diverting the time vector to a new direction.

Among new cities, capital cities have symbolic values that attract particular attention. Although the twentieth century saw an unprecedented establishment of new capitals, the creation of a city where none existed before is infrequent. And among the capital cities created from scratch, Brasília still stands out 50 years after its inauguration in 1960. Kenneth Frampton (2010: 20) recently considered that 'none of the modern capital cities founded after the Second World War can quite equal Brasília for the monumental, geomantic character of its conception and for the subsequent speed of its systematic realization.' What makes Brasília a monument of the modern city is more than its built environment (the combination of its plan and architecture), but rather a unique idea of urbanity that finally came to life.

Brasília

Jean-Loup Herbert (2006: 17), when writing about Brasília, asked rhetorically whether it would be possible to build a city without streets, façades, urban fabric or place. This was partially what Lucio Costa and Oscar Niemeyer intended to do, by questioning the formal elements usually considered part of the cityscape, as well as questioning the form of the city, and proposing a new form of urbanity; they selected which elements should be taken into account which were not prevalent in other urban plans but were already reshaping urban life, and designed how to arrange them spatially, propelling a modern urban society.

To a certain extent, Brasília is the apex of urban ideologies and design principles that had been discussed for decades, theoretically based on Le Corbusier's ideas. Despite the direct influence, including Le Corbusier's brief participation in Lucio Costa's project for the Brazilian Ministry of Education and Health in 1936, Herbert (2006) points out that there are no explicit references to Le Corbusier's Chandigarh in Brasília. Instead, the new Brazilian capital presents a mix of many other modern influences, from urban highways that were redesigning North American cities to traits of the garden cities and communal life of Soviet constructivism. In fact, Brazil's modernist architecture had already acquired a character of its own, which was the theme of an exhibition at the Museum of Modern Art in New York, in 1943.

In Brasília, Lucio Costa's plan and Oscar Niemeyer's buildings are drenched in symbolism and monumentality: modern functions of the city were one important aspect of their proposals, but not the crux of their design. Oscar Niemeyer (1966: 21) actually criticized 'some circles in

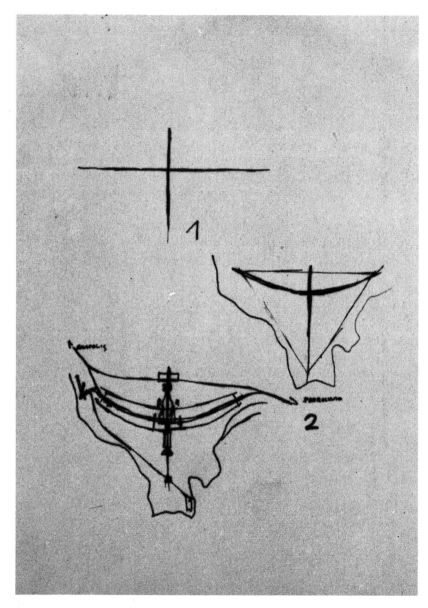

Figure 6.1 Lucio Costa, *Sketches for Brasília*, 1955 © Arquivo Público do Distrito Federal

Conceiving the city 119

modern architecture' that voluntarily 'feel safer and more at ease when limited by rules and regulations', which 'lead them to passively accept solutions that, repeated again and again, become almost vulgar'. For Niemeyer, architecture may convey emotions, and a 'mood ecstasy, of dreams, of poetry'.

Brasília was built in less than 4 years. Lucio Costa's proposal was selected in March 1957, and the capital was dedicated on 21 April 1960, an emblematic date in Brazil, where it marks the death of Tiradentes, a barber and revolutionary who fought Portuguese rule over the country in the eighteenth century.

In the late 1950s, there were no roads from the main cities to the construction site, which was also emblematically located in the middle of the country, roughly 1,000 kilometres from the coast and the cities of São Paulo, Belo Horizonte, Salvador and Rio de Janeiro, which was the capital at that time. Machines, building material and personnel initially had to be flown to Brasília; only after a highway system was built could everything be trucked in. Contemporary aerial images of the expanses of the Brazilian *cerrado* travelled the world, showing the geopolitical and urbanistic audacity of Brasília. In the midst of dusty soil and twisted vegetation, a clear cross was drawn on the ground, then a single white sculptural palace arose and slowly the capital of the modernistic urban ideal emerged. Even today, when Brasília's airport is one of the busiest in the country, it is thrilling to glimpse the layout of the *Plano Piloto*, now not alone among the vast, dry and dusty *cerrado*, but nestled amid several other cities where the urban fabric (and social fabric as well) is so similar to that of any other poor Brazilian city, and so different from Brasília.

When Brasília was inaugurated, only 20 percent of the city had been completed (Stenzel and Dorfman, 2011). Then, as today, there were more people living in the outskirts of the city than within the *Plano Piloto*, in a mix of planned, improvised and often slum-like townships. Fifty years after its inauguration, unlike any of Brazil's state capitals, where the core city tends to present higher population densities, these peripheral cities still have higher population densities than Brasília. Brasília's metropolitan region conjures four characteristics: fragmentation, dispersion, socio-spatial segregation and eccentricity – meaning that only the functional centre of the metropolitan region is located in the capital, whereas the demographic and morphological centres reside in neighbouring areas which were not part of the original plan (Holanda, 2010: 47).

For its importance as the icon of the modernist city, for envisioning how the city of the future could be, Brasília brings rich material to support the analysis of how space was conceived, how territory has been used to enforce political, social and urbanistic ideas, and how places have been

120 Conceiving the city

created as tentative acts of affective appropriation of space within the modernist city.

Space in Brasília

Brasília embodies a particular idea of a city. In the site chosen for the new capital, there were almost no topographical constraints to be taken into account, and certainly no architectural or urban references. Rio de Janeiro was hundreds of kilometres south, the closest town was inexpressive and the few materializations of modernist urban principles were separated by an ocean and insurmountable time scales. All of this gave Lucio Costa and Oscar Niemeyer the opportunity not only to design a city, but also to design and build an idea of the urban future.

Space is composed of the relations between entities and flows strained by sensorial and cultural filters. By proposing a capital city for the future, Costa and Niemeyer emphasized specific entities and flows, which would also demand the adaptation of the sensorial and cultural filters of future inhabitants. Reading Costa's entry in the competition to design the new Brazilian capital can give us some hints about how he envisioned the new city.

Costa's plan for Brasília competed with twenty-five other entries. His entry begins with a mix of humility ('It was not my intention to enter the competition – nor, indeed, am I really doing so,' is his opening phrase) and a demiurgic approach ('I am merely liberating my mind from a possible solution which sprang to it as a complete picture, but one which I had not sought.') His epic rhetoric, notes James Holston (1989: 65), 'dehistoricizes it by presenting it in the terms of a foundation myth, divinely inspired'.

His was the only self-contained plan, not open to further and spontaneous growth. This self-containment lent an iconic aura to the plan, which was centred on two crossed axes, with one of them curved to fit the topography and an imaginary equilateral triangle, which made the basic urban structure resemble an airplane. Sixty *superquadras* (superblocks) were arranged along the north-south axis; each of these contained roughly eighteen six-story blocks which were supposed to work as mini-communities. The ministerial buildings flank the east-west axis, and a wide lawn separates its two expressways. At the crossing of the axes is a complex urban structure which includes viaducts connecting the axes, parking areas and the bus terminal. The focal point of the plan is the Plaza of the Three Powers (judiciary, executive and legislative), which is also the symbolic centre of the country.

Perhaps the single element that defines Brasília's design, not only on the city scale but also on the human scale, is the car. Costa envisioned a

Conceiving the city 121

symbiotic relationship between cars and people. Indeed, the first urban structure mentioned in Costa's proposal is the highway. After general guidelines on how the highways would function as the backbone of the plan, and 'once a network for motorized traffic had been established, an independent grid of safe-transit footpaths for pedestrians had to be organized' (Costa, 1960: 53). The car would be an essential entity in the city of the future; Costa argued that it had already been 'domesticated and is almost a member of the family' (*ibid.*).

Although cars are an essential feature of Brasília, it seems that Lucio Costa only thought of them as flows, disregarding what would happen when they reached their destination. There were not enough parking spaces in the original plan (Evenson, 1973), and the situation has worsened as motorization rates currently reach 40 vehicles per 100 people in the metropolitan region, among the highest in the country.

In many ways, Brasília represents the apotheosis of the modern technological world that acquired economic, political and cultural dimensions in the first half of the twentieth century. Evenson (1973: 151) sees the 'glorification of the machine' in a still relatively unindustrialized country reaching extremes, to the point that Brazilians were proud of building an 'entire city to the scale of the motor', and even defacing natural features (such as Rio de Janeiro's beachfronts) with wide avenues and fast-moving traffic. To move the core of civic life away from the huge lake created at the site which would receive the capital and to centre it along two highway axes and modernist buildings is a statement that the character of the city would arise from itself, and not from any external reference. As if the modernist city was only possible if it gave birth to itself.

Ten years after the inauguration of Brasília, Costa (1970) wrote an important short text: 'The urban planner defends his capital.' Costa starts by claiming that Brasília does not represent an individual whim, but a collect project of a nation that was heading towards the future, and emphasizes the collective 'people', which was dedicated to constructing a 'new Brazil, a people resolutely oriented to the future' (Costa, 1970: 7). In this sense, creating the space of the future demanded Lucio Costa to challenge existing sensorial, technological, and cultural filters, and to emphasize entities and flows that were alien or would be disruptive in other cities at that time. And as Leonardo Benevolo (1999: 764) pointed out, Niemeyer's architecture is what gives shape to Costa's plan – the plan and buildings creating a new urban space. A space has been conceived as a representation of power, which through urban design and architecture has to be constantly reiterated. Niemeyer's poetic architecture serves as a marvellous camouflage for a totalitarian space, which leaves no room for spatial improvisation.

122 Conceiving the city

Territory in Brasília

The idea of relocating the capital of Brazil to the interior of the country was first raised in the late-eighteenth century by both Portugal and those who advocated for Brazilian sovereignty. For Portugal, an inland capital would assure that the country would remain under its control, and would also protect the colony from marine attacks on Rio de Janeiro. For the revolutionaries of Minas Gerais, who fought for independence from Portugal, a new capital represented a symbolic detachment from the colony (Evenson, 1973). Seventy years after Brazil's independence, in 1822, the Republican constitution secured an area of 14,400 square kilometres in the central plateau area to create the new capital, which by then had already been baptized Brasília. A team comprised a doctor, a botanist, a geographer, a geologist and a landscape architect mapped the area and defined the location of the future capital. But the idea of moving the national capital remained dormant until the 1950s, when president Juscelino Kubitscheck made the construction of Brasília the flagship project of his government and of his strategy to turn Brazil into a modern nation, leap-frogging several economic and social steps to turn the country into an industrial player under the slogan 'fifty years in five'.

Despite the long gestation of the idea of moving the capital inland, it is not surprising that when the time came, the move was controversial; politicians and journalists were divided between those who endorsed the idea as a move away from the traditional and pernicious political environment centred in Rio de Janeiro and their counterparts, who argued the move was a fantasy that would cost the future of the country. Gilberto Freyre (1960), one of the most important Brazilian sociologists, was a vocal critic of Brasília. He criticized the emphasis on technocracy, arguing that the typical easygoing nature of *cariocas* (residents of Rio de Janeiro) was how the country would make a difference in the world, and that the proposed plan was more like an architectural sculpture that did not consider the country's complex social, economic and cultural dimensions. Indeed, Lucio Costa (1960) said that building Brasília was a matter of 'taking possession of a place' and 'imposing upon it, as the conquerors or Louis XIV had done previously, an urban structure', which would become a capital city (Costa, 1970: 8).

Only a few years after Brasília's inauguration came an event which was decisive for the full establishment of the capital: the military coup of 1964. The military entrenched itself in the city, controlling the country far from economic, political and social pressures from the main cities of São Paulo and Rio de Janeiro. The monumental scales of Brasília's plan and its official buildings may also have played an important role for the military dictatorship, with regard to the 'military fondness of ceremony

Conceiving the city   123

and nationalist symbols' (Everson, 1973: 165). Territories require strong symbols to convey a message, to shape a coherent identity that does not include shades of gray. Brasília's clean layout and architectural monuments perfectly fit this purpose.

In the centre of the country, Brasília became the focal point of a new system of highways. These new road connections between regions, in a country that was simultaneously dismantling its railway system and investing in oil extraction, were designed to unify a nation that was overly controlled by a central power.

On the metropolitan scale, the self-contained plan immediately reinforced territorial divisions which were common in other Brazilian cities, with the destitute living on the outskirts not enjoying the benefits of the formal and planned city. Costa (1970: 7), when defending his plan, said his intention with the *superquadras* was to promote a social mix, and blamed 'administrative inaptitude' for not fulfilling this 'fundamental aspect' of the plan. Niemeyer (1970: 10), on the same occasion, said he was disappointed with the social cleavage that he could see in Brasília, repeating the 'misery and social contrasts' one could find anywhere in the country.

One must respect Costa's and Niemeyer's opinions about their own work. Nevertheless, this social mixing is not clearly proposed in the original document presented by Costa, and even if it was intended, it either reveals their sincere idealism or profound naiveté with regard to the social and urban fabric of Brazil. Both then and now, in Brazil and virtually anywhere and at any time in history – from New York's 1811 grid to Mumbai's slums and non-notified areas – planned and legal urban parcels are an important real estate asset which has the immediate effect of increasing land prices and consequently pricing out the poor. In the case of Brasília, which was inaugurated with 80 per cent of its population already occupying the satellite towns, a territorial schism was congenital to the plan. Some apartments built in the *superquadras* at the very beginning of its construction already exposed 'the vicious features of a town dominated by speculators' (Wilheim, 1960: 38), and despite the discourse of egalitarianism, the apartment buildings featured minuscule, windowless rooms for domestic employees. As Norman Evenson (1973: 174) puts it, despite Costa's and Niemeyer's criticism regarding the lack of social mix within the *Plano Piloto*, 'Brasília would have failed to achieve its image of an ideal modern environment if it had not embodied a high standard of living.'

In an acrid observation, James Holston (1989: 29) points out, 'These disparities suggest that the successes of Brasília's order depend to a considerable degree upon keeping the forces of disorder out of the capital and in the periphery.' And as Jeferson Tavares (2004: 59) has observed,

124 Conceiving the city

Brasília 'seduced by its novelty and sinned by its traditions': the core planned city is surrounded by an 'uncontrolled' periphery. In order to maintain its aura of a novel urban space, Brasília (its architecture as well as its urban design and metropolitan development) resorted to traditional territorial instruments, with the urbanist and the architect often trying to elude any responsibility.

Place in Brasília

Brasília was initially a placeless city. In her famous phrase 'There is no there there,' Gertrude Stein[1] reflected her nostalgia when she visited Oakland after an absence of more than 30 years and did not find her family's home. She had lost her sense of place regarding her hometown. 'There' not only indicates location, but also time; Stein's inexistent 'there' is a place which had disappeared with the passage of time, a place she cannot find where it existed before. If 'there' has the multi-temporal character of being before, after and simultaneously elsewhere, 'here' is encapsulated by the present. Layers of historical objects, tales and values are commonly merged in any 'here'. 'Here' is often a historically dense present. If 'there' was no longer located in Stein's Oakland, we could say there was no 'here' when Brasília was inaugurated. There was nobody before Brasília. And everybody who came to Brasília came from somewhere else.

Clarice Lispector (2015), an important Brazilian fiction writer, chronicled Brasília's early years. Her first story after visiting the city in 1962 starts: 'Brasília is artificial. As artificial as the world must have been when it was created.' She continues: 'It is urgent: if it doesn't get populated, or rather overpopulated, it will be too late: there will be no place for people. They will be tacitly expelled.' Visiting the city 12 years later, her impression had not changed much: 'Brasília is an abstract city. And there is no way to make it concrete. (. . .) In Brasília there is practically nowhere to drop dead.'

Jânio Quadros, who served as Brazil's president for only 7 months before resigning in August 1961, wrote an ironic op-ed letter addressed to the general director of the postal and telegraph services after he realized that several letters addressed to him had been returned to the sender 'because the postal staff do not know my address'[2] (Chaia and Chaia, 2011). Brasília's 'here' was to be formed not by the overlay of objects, values and people of different times that shared the same portion of space, but by everybody and anybody who came from somewhere else.

Lawrence Vale (2006: 26) argues that 'the functionless openness of the government axis and plazas seems more likely to attract architectural photographers than social citizenry.' Indeed, Brasília is an equally

Figure 6.2 Brasília – Ministério em Construção, 1958 © Instituto Moreira Salles

attractive and challenging subject for photographers. Marcel Gautherot (Frampton, Gautherot, 2010) spent decades in Brazil and closely followed the construction of the capital. The ethereal skeletons of burgeoning buildings constructed of steel and concrete seem to float over the dusty and vast landscape. Just as impressive as these monumental photos are Gautherot's portraits of the newcomers. Each of them looks confidently at the camera, often with a timid smile – some working to construct the capital, others building their own wooden houses, which do not bear a single sign indicating they are in Brasília. While the capital's architectural monuments have the cloudscapes of Brazil's central plateau as their background, at the human level the background of the portraits is twisted and almost leafless trees.

126 *Conceiving the city*

René Burri (2011) has also documented the arrival of the people who would eventually populate Brasília, or more precisely, who would populate the outskirts of the city. Yet the monumentality of the city is inescapable. From Roberto Burle Marx's landscaped organic gardens to the cloverleaf crossings and wide roadways and Oscar Niemeyer's architectural monuments, people appear here and there in Burri's photographs. Sometimes it is a solitary soldier guarding an empty modernist palace, sometimes buses upon buses pouring out some of the 30,000 workers who travelled thousands of miles, leaving everything behind to build the new capital. A representative photo shows a family, parents and four children. Under the arches of the Presidential Palace, the children and wife look at the building with astonishment and awe, accompanied by the proud father, who may have worked to build the city. But it is more likely that Brasília was not a place for them. After their short visit, they would head off to the so-called satellite cities, which at that time already resembled ordinary small and impoverished Brazilian cities.

In contrast, there is nobody in Lina Kim and Michael Wesely's (2011) photos of Brasília. The feeling is that of a ghost city: either abandoned by its inhabitants, or still waiting to be populated. Empty multiple-lane avenues without sidewalks framing yellowish lawns with medium-sized, distorted trees typical of the Brazilian *cerrado*, where the rectangular ministry buildings are located. Their narrow façades of pure concrete, and the larger ones covered with metal and glass panels, mark the regular rhythm of the monumental axis, peppered with magisterial architectural follies such as Brasília's cathedral or the national congress. And yet, in another depopulated photo, a huge concrete residential building in the *superquadras* is the backdrop for a humble news stand that also functions as a fax booth, DVD rental shop and office supply store. While the newsstand represents a minute and spontaneous appropriation of space in the middle of the planned city, both the newsstand and building are sided by a tall, wide and (most likely) old tree. Keeping in mind Brasília's archetypal image as an abstract city, a city with the future before it but with no past, the contradictions of this image are overwhelming: a news stand draws its strength from its frailty and inexpressiveness, before the modernist façade, or a tree that seems to be older than the beginning of the modern city. Suddenly one notes that places might emerge in the middle of the abstract space of the modernist city.

In an interview with Alex Shoumatoff (1987: 39), Lucio Costa said he suggested that each *superquadra* be planted with different trees to instill a sense of place, and that the community-like approach to the *superquadras* was supposed to promote social interactions.

Architects and urbanists interviewed in the documentary made by Mário Salimon and Marcelo Feijó (2014) about Brasília make the point that Costa's *superquadras* are three times lower and spatially more compressed than the twenty-story high and endlessly aligned housing towers proposed by Le Corbusier and other modern architects. Some of the interviewees even liken the morphology of the *superquadras* to the urbanity of small cities, which would never be found in the massive modernist housing projects. But they also recognize that Brasília created ghettos for rich families, and that the architectural and urban uniformity of the *superquadras* removes the necessary diversity that creates empathies with the city. Indeed, the first inhabitants of Brasília who moved from other cities found that the lack of street life – sidewalks, corners, shopping façades, human-scale public spaces – produced 'not just an interiorization of social encounters, but also a profound sense of isolation' (Holston, 1989: 107).

Any attempt to create places in the modernist city would have to wait a few more years, when its inhabitants would appropriate portions of space with affective values. Place does not need to have a past, but a history, even if it is the history of the future. The construction of places is fundamentally full of nuances, contradictions and individualities. The masterminds of the modernist city, who favoured homogeneous and overarching values, could not mandate the construction of places. Today, in some areas of the *Plano Piloto,* predetermined uses have been reverted, and unexpected appropriation of spaces can be seen in the daily life of *brasilienses* – the people born and raised in the city of the future. Individuals and groups who were not even imagined in the original plan use the city in unexpected ways (Nunes, 2009).

Visiting the *superquadras* today, it is possible to see several small deviations, in a delicate balance between preserving the undeniable importance of Costa's and Niemeyer's *oeuvre*, and attempting to imprint individual values of identity onto a portion of space.

It is when the future becomes present, when a makeshift news stand and a tree which is unexpectedly older than the city share the same portion of space and bring different timescales to the modernist space, that places finally blossom in Brasília. In a self-contained and mythical space, enforced by layers of symbolic territories, creating places becomes a subversive act.

Notes

1. Stein, Gertrude (1937) *Everybody's Autobiography.* New York, NY: Random House.
2. In *O Estado de S. Paulo,* 6 July, 1961.

128 Conceiving the city

References

Benevolo, Leonardo (1999) *History of modern architecture* (Vol 2). Cambridge, MA: MIT Press (© 1977).

Burri, René (2011) *Brasilia*. Zurich: Scheidegger & Spiess.

Chaia, Miguel; Chaia, Vera (2011) Brasília's political dimension. In: Kim, Lina; Wesely, Michael (eds) *Archiv Utopia | Archive Utopia*. Kiel: Kunsthalle zu Kiel, 155–161.

Costa, Lucio (1960) Plano Piloto de Brasília. Brasília 1960: Uma interpretação. *Acrópole: Brasília* – special issue 256/257.

Costa, Lucio (1970) O urbanista defende a sua capital. *Acrópole,* 32(375–376): 7–9.

Evenson, Norma (1973) *Two Brazilian capitals: Architecture and urbanism in Rio de Janeiro and Brasília.* New Haven, CT: Yale University Press.

Frampton, Kenneth; Gautherot, Marcel (2010) *Building Brasília*. London: Thames & Hudson.

Freyre, Gilberto (1960) *Brasil, Brasis, Brasília*. Rio de Janeiro: Record.

Herbert, Jean-Loup (2006) Brasilia, l'épanouissement d'une capitale. In: Monnier, Gérard (ed) *Brasilia, l'épanouissement d'une capitale*. Paris: Picard; 17–40.

Holanda, Frederico de (2010) *Brasília: cidade moderna, cidade eternal.* Brasília: FAU UnB.

Holston, James (1989) *The modernist city. An anthropological critique of Brasília.* Chicago, IL: Chicago University Press.

Kim, Lina; Wesely, Michael (2011) *Archiv Utopia | Archive Utopia*. Kiel: Kunsthalle zu Kiel.

Lispector, Clarice (2015) *The complete stories.* New York, NY: New Directions (Translated by Katrina Dodson).

Niemeyer, Oscar (1966) "Oscar Niemeyer thoughts on Brasília". In: Stäubli, Willy. *Brasília*. Stuttgart: Alexander Koch, 21–23.

Niemeyer, Oscar (1970) Brasília 70. *Acrópole,* 32(375–76): 10–11.

Nunes, Brasilmar Ferreira (2009) Elementos para uma sociologia dos espaços edificados em cidades: o "Conic" no Plano Piloto de Brasília. *Cadernos Metrópole,* 21(1): 13–32.

Salimon, Mário; Feijó, Marcelo (2014) *Superquadras* [Documentary Film]. At http://superquadras.org

Shoumatoff, Alex (1987) *The Capital of hope – Brasília and its people.* Albuquerque: University of New Mexico Press.

Stenzel, Emilia; Dorfman, Gabriel (2011) "Brasília of the city as a work of art". In: Kim, Lina; Wesely, Michael. *Archiv Utopia | Archive Utopia*. Kiel: Kunsthalle zu Kiel; 48–55.

Tavares, Jeferson (2004) *Projetos para Brasília e a cultura urbanística nacional* – Dissertação de Mestrado: Universidade de São Paulo.

Vale, Lawrence (2006) Seven types of capital city. In: Gordon, David. *Planning Twentieth Century Capital Cities.* New York, NY: Routledge; 15–37.

Wilheim, Jorge (1960) Brasília 1960: Uma interpretação. *Acrópole: Brasília* – special issue 256/257.

7 Conceiving the city
What is next?

Adding, carving, weaving

Spaces, places and territories are created, destroyed and recreated daily. Not only are we defined by the position we occupy in space at different moments (which, as discussed previously, encompasses specific and changing relations we establish with places and territories), but we also become what we are as individuals and social groups by the creation, destruction and recreation of spaces, places and territories. In a process that there is no beginning, we construct spaces that shape us as individuals and society.

The cycle of creating, destroying and recreating spaces extends over intervals that vary from daily activities to historical periods. Sometimes this creation cycle does not leave any trace, but in other situations it becomes physically impregnated in the terrain and in people's minds for generations.

In cafes around the world, everyday people choose tables, open up laptops or books, arrange their belongings, reposition tables and chairs, work and chat, and create temporary places – portions of space they take possession of provisionally through personal objects, signs and behaviours. After they are gone, their places vanish. Other people arrive and the cycle starts anew. Sometimes, although the construction of places leaves no permanent traces in the physical space, it creates a deep and personal attachment between an individual and a portion of space. As Raimund Gregorius, the main character in the novel *Night Train to Lisbon* says, 'We leave something of ourselves behind when we leave a place. We stay there even though we go away. And there are things in us that we can find again only by going back there' (Mercier, 2008: 243). And sometimes this affective and cultural appropriation of portions of space impregnates and physically transforms the landscape. Bill Hillier and Laura Vaughan (2007) analyzed the physical features of Nicosia, capital of Cyprus, which has very distinct Greek and Turkish enclaves.

130 *Conceiving the city: what is next?*

Using a methodology Hillier pioneered, called space syntax, which calculates the integration of each road segment with every other in a city, the authors found impregnated in space deep cultural characteristics of both peoples. In the Greek section, the streets follow a linear grid with more integration between the roads, while in the Turkish quarter there is less road integration and shorter streets, which would be more akin to cities in the Islamic world. Layers of cultural appropriations of a space that share the same geological and environmental substratum have been accumulating over time, to the point that place making, which is *a priori* an affective appropriation of a portion of space, changes the physical features of space.

Whether ephemeral or long lasting, the previous examples show cycles of creation, destruction and recreation of spaces, places and territories that occur spontaneously. But there are also intentional cycles, when new spatial ideas are tested. We discussed Brasília in the previous chapter because its urban plan and architecture pushed the boundaries of what urban space could be. On the one hand, Brasília was the materialization of urban ideas that had been maturing for decades as part of the modernist movement. On the other hand, Brasília was a starting point: for the first time, a complete city built upon modernist principles would be inhabited by a large number of people, by a complex society. Which spaces, places and territories would emerge from this intersection between an idea of a modernist city and its inhabitants was an open question. And as we have seen, especially the construction of places took time. What would come after Brasília?

Unfortunately, cities in developed and developing countries suffered from a reductionist approach of modernist urban principles. Although polemical, the brilliance of Le Corbusier's ideas, the elegance of Costa's plan, the irreverence of Niemeyer's architecture (to use the same examples) were replaced by a narrow view of the modern city as a functional city. City planning, in many cases, had been reduced to zoning plans: a collection of rules determining which urban functions (commerce, industry, housing) should be located where, following a set of occupation rules (building heights, setbacks, etc.). And contradictory as it may seem, those rules were often formless. If Le Corbusier's ideas intended to push urbanistic thinking forward, challenging the traditional organization and aesthetic of the city, city planning via zoning pulled urbanistic thinking backward: setting rules that ultimately would freeze space in the present (of that time), not questioning or proposing new ways of creating space.

This is why Henri Lefebvre (2014: 03) includes architecture and landscape as core disciplines for creating spaces in the city, and leaves out planning on purpose. Dominated by the instruments of 'land use planning (. . .) certain agents and powers intervene that are quite capable of crushing architects and their work completely, if only by putting them in a subordinate position, by confining them to the mere execution of a program'. The vindication of a scientific and quantitative approach to urban planning had been misappropriated to justify land use planning. However, this might as well have been an excuse 'of designers to give up the more complex structures of traditional cities, characterized by the experience of overlap, ambiguity, multiplicity' (Stanek, 2011: 105).

In the context of this book, we could say that the modernist city intended to create a novel understanding and experience of space, incorporating new entities and flows, while land-use planning considers the city in territorial terms, shaping urban space through a set of rules; finally, movements such as the New Urbanism aim to creating places by designing them through well-established architectural references and community values. Although the artificiality of creating territories and places prior to the actual experience of space seems awkward (if not repulsive), any attempt to create spaces, places and territories yields the intentionality to change the character of an existing reality through spatial interventions. Specifically through the practice of architecture, Michael Hays (2010: 01) writes that it is a way of 'negotiating the real (. . .) a specific kind of socially symbolic production whose primary task is the construction of concepts and subject positions rather than the making of things'.

Indeed, questioning existing spatialities and proposing new ones is a constitutive trait of professional city makers – and here I am mostly referring to architects, urban designers and landscape architects. We can consider the construction of urban spaces, places and territories as made of three processes: adding, carving and weaving. In these three processes, intentionality is key. This despite the fact that these city makers know their works will ultimately be either destroyed or incorporated into the urban fabric to the point of being indistinguishable from their contexts, and even when city makers intently argue for this ephemeral aspect of space, they are physically building up their ideas in the city.

Adding is the most obvious process of creating more (not necessarily new) urban spaces, places and territories. This encompasses physical and conceptual addition by either actually building more cities over existing cities or laying out a plan that induces the creation of space according to certain principles. The 1811-plan for Manhattan is an example of conceptual urban addition. Conceived by Simeon De Witt, Gouverneur Morris and John Rutherfurd, the regular grid encompassing more than 2,000 new regular city blocks would facilitate and give security to real estate developers. It would also transform New York topography radically, by 'leveling rugged terrain, which ranged as high as 154 feet

132 *Conceiving the city: what is next?*

above sea level; burying rippling streams, glistering ponds, and green marsh; and creating one gargantuan drainage dilemma' (Stenberg, 2014: 42). Rem Khoolaas (1994: 19) called the plan 'the most courageous act of prediction in Western civilization'.

More recently, China has become the prime example of physical addition of space. After the 1978 Cultural Revolution and especially during the rapid economic growth of the early-twenty-first century, China added and has continued to add urban spaces to its existing cities and rural areas at a vertiginous pace. Looking at the new towns of Ordos, Kunming or Xinyang, or the copycat cities of Little Paris in Tianducheng and Florentia Village in Wuqing, it is impossible to see any concern with the future of these cities – or with the future of cities in general, in a more conceptual and forwarding way, but only the addition of more cities for the future. Hundreds of thousands of empty housing and office buildings await urbanization that will inevitably come, a type of urbanization that will only replicate the same spatial logic that already exists. Adding, as a method of creating space, rarely has the strength to propose new forms of urbanity. Replicating existing urban models is the fastest way to keep pace with rapid urbanization and slows down any innovative approach to urban design.

The construction of more cities reflects the demographic expansion that is occurring now in Asia and the Persian Gulf, as once happened in Europe and North America. Despite the showiness of the Chinese thematic cities, Gulf cities seem to make any additional space a symbolic act. Dubai, Abu Dhabi and other Gulf city-states import cheap labour from neighbouring poor countries as part of their strategy to become attractive global *entrepôts* and points of entry to global markets. In some of the Gulf states, urbanization makes the addition of space a geographic and environmental endeavour, with artificial islands in various shapes and sizes, indoor ski slopes, and carefully trimmed lawns in the desert irrigated all year round – Dubai consumes 500 litres per capita a capital, three times higher than the European consumption. Even in model cities such as Masdar, designed by Norman Foster to promote sustainable urban solutions, the social complexities of a real city are put aside. Engaging technologists, consultants and investors in its conception, it is a stepping-stone and showcase for green solutions – while workers, again brought from abroad to build the city, will have no place this showcase city. Indeed, some of the plans for the new Chinese and Gulf cities seem to endorse and expand Alan Hess's (1993: np) statement that 'Las Vegas and Disneyland are the two most potent urban models in twentieth-century America.'

Carving happens when an existing space is transformed, when new spatialities are created within consolidated spatial organizations; and

Conceiving the city: what is next? 133

weaving occurs when some elements are introduced with the main goal of connecting otherwise unrelated pieces of the urban space. Both processes can take place on different scales, from the neighbourhood to the world. The occupation of long-vacant industrial warehouses is an example of carving spaces that happens by reintegrating these spaces into the urban fabric. In the 1980s, the international competition to design the Park of La Villette at the former site of several slaughterhouses and the national wholesale meat market marked an age of important urban reconstructions. Hays (2010: 155) likens Bernard Tschumi's programmatic design of La Villette to 'a kind of architectural DNA: all of the information necessary for the generation and organization of a fully functioning set of programmatic-spatial events is present, but none of the substance'. And Charles Waldheim (2016: 16) sees in the project the reassurance of 'landscape as the most suitable medium through which to order programmatic and social change over time, especially complex evolving arrangements of urban activities'.

Urban infrastructures have been labelled as residual spaces and non-places. True, they give life to urban settings – they literally oxygenate, illuminate and circulate urban flows. But their functional existence, bearing no social or cultural appropriation, makes urban infrastructures be often deemed as second-class spaces. Moreover when their core function has lost importance as the supporting skeleton of the city – this is what happened with aqueducts, urban railways and waterways, or warehouses and gas tanks. Their removal from space is not as simple as putting down energy cables and tracks once used for trams. They leave urban scars. They are the least noble areas of brownfields. They are the uppermost void within non-places.

However, precisely for being more resistant to urban changes, they bear the memory of an era when the city was the engine of the industrial economy. Architects, planners, artists and urban advocates have been repurposing these areas. They have been carving exciting new places in these infrastructural, and not seldom derelict and despised urban spaces. The conversion of the gasometer in Oberhausen as the cultural centre of the Ruhr region in Germany, a stretch of an abandoned railway in Paris reclaimed as an urban park in the *Promenade Plantée*, or more recently the conversion of a freight railroad running through Manhattan in the High Line park, are examples of urban renewals based on infrastructural spaces. As Ryan Gravel (2016: 141) points out, these transformations 'can be even sexy (. . .) seductive (. . .) muscular (. . .) sensual – infrastructure forms the physical and sensory space in which we live our lives. (. . .) Infrastructure gets us home in time for dinner, lights our way on a romantic stroll, and draws our bath for a quiet evening at home without the kids'.

134 *Conceiving the city: what is next?*

Weaving is focused on relating existing elements of urban spaces, usually with the introduction of other elements. The goal is to connect, or reconnect, unrelated pieces of the urban space. It ranges from large infrastructures that weave regions through often-invisible techno-logical networks (from sewer to electricity and the Internet) to more delicate urban interventions. This is the case in Medellín, Colombia, where the hilly poor neighbourhoods, once home to powerful drug dealers and devoid of urban services, have been reconnected to the city through transportation links based on cable cars and escalators. Since the early 2000s, the area has also received parks, schools and public libraries, which brought international recognition to the city and awards to architects, such as Giancarlo Mazzanti, designer of the España Library Park. Weaving becomes particularly challenging as well as exciting with the ubiquitous presence of information and communi-cation technologies. The miniaturization of electronic and digital devices allows them to be embedded in objects that form the urban structure and buildings, to become pervasive in the urban fabric – and, still, to pass unnoticed. Electronic devices are not anymore attached to buildings, but are rather integral parts of them. The same process that once happened with technologies such as water supply and electricity, which were appendices to the buildings and became constituents of their infra-structure, screens, thermostats, lighting controls and several other devices are becoming intrinsic elements of architecture. The spread of wireless communication networks turned every device into a communication node, making the design of the relationships between close and distant objects and flows part of the architectural creative and building process. And the groundbreaking works in material sciences allow bricks and mortar, glasses and walls, to be programmable in accordance to the willing of the dwellers, and responsive to the internal and external environments. As William Mitchell (1996: 104) had advanced in the 1990s, 'building and parts of buildings must now be related not only to their natural and urban contexts, but also to their cyberspace settings'. Creating these relations and weaving the physical and digital spatial elements are transforming the urban space.

Similar to this book's core concepts of space, place and territory, adding, carving and weaving are not related to measurable dimensions. Likewise, there is seldom a clear-cut limit between these processes. Ultimately, adding, carving and weaving are inherent processes of creating urban spaces, places and territories. Brasília has been highlighted as the landmark of urbanization through the addition of space. In order to discuss carving and weaving, I focus on two other urban elements: the Berlin Wall and airports.

The Berlin Wall

Roughly one year after Brasília was inaugurated, another urban intervention consolidated the city as a central component of the twentieth-century. Why such an iconic component of recent urban history is mostly absent from books on urban theory or the history of cities is still open to debate. On the night of 13 August 1961, the East German government decided to curtail movement between East and West Berlin. A fence became a wall, and the wall became a 100 metre wide no-man's land peppered with watchtowers. The Berlin Wall arguably became one of the most powerful territorial devices of modern history, and a defining element in urban design.

Walls had been a common architectural element for centuries. They were used to encircle the city against its surroundings, defining those who deserved protection against the outside world and restricting commercial and social privileges to those living within the walls. But by the mid-twentieth-century, walls were urban relics. At that time, East and West Germany were parts of the socialist and capitalist geopolitical spheres. East Germany was sealed off from Western Europe since 1952. Fearing total Soviet control during the 1950s, hundreds of thousands of East Germans fled to West Germany every year through Berlin, an open enclave in the middle of the Soviet bloc, whose borderline laid 200 kilometres to the west. Yet the physical separation of East and West Berlin through the wall dividing the historical capital of Germany took Berliners – and the world – by surprise. A 140-km-long border was drawn through the city, crossing areas of housing, industries, woods, waterways, railways and marshland. The wall encircled West Berlin, turning the open enclave with East Germany into what Pier Vittorio Aureli (2011: 223) perceived as 'a closed island within a hostile territory, making any flights to the suburbs impossible'. West Berlin population steadily declined in the 1970s, and whole quarters were depopulated and abandoned. Aureli analyzes Oswald Mathias Ungers's project *Green Archipelago*, which concentrated efforts in developing only parts of the city, and even promoting the demolition of abandoned ones. The selection of these 'islands' was based 'on the possibility of discerning what had developed over time as cornerstones of the symbolic geography of the city' (Aureli, 2011: 223). And perhaps more radical in Ungers project is what he proposed to leave in between these urban islands: vast green areas, agricultural land and forests, to be left free of any designed or enforced development.

However insightful such proposals might have been, the wall physically and symbolically reshaped the urbanity of Berlin. As often happens with territorial devices, the Berlin Wall became a keystone for defining and

136　*Conceiving the city: what is next?*

enforcing Eastern and Western 'Germanness'. Delineated by two conflicting worldviews, the socialist and capitalist governments of East and West Germany used the wall as a symbol of the differences that characterized each part of Berlin (and each country), mostly using opposing values. As discussed earlier, they conveyed an illusion of *place identity* to enforce territorial dominance. As Emily Pugh (2014: 31) states, 'Berlin was a central site wherein each government attempted to articulate a national identity that distanced it from the Nazi regime and proved it was the true and rightful Germany.' In West Berlin, painting graffiti on the wall became an expression of discontentment with local and global issues, and the fact that a significant part of the graffiti was in English indicates that the wall was also used as a canvas to the world.

As unexpectedly as it was constructed, the Berlin Wall was destroyed on the night of 9 November 1989. Days of jubilant demolition followed, and the no-man's land was occupied. Pieces of the wall were collected and sold as souvenirs, mostly by 'the marginals of German society (students, pensioners, and Polish, Italian, or Turkish *Gastarbeiter*' (Baker, 2005: 32). In January 1990, the East German government promoted the painting of the wall on its side, and began to sell pieces of it to museums, galleries and private collectors worldwide. Four years after the fall, 'less is left of the Berlin Wall than of Hadrian's Wall' (Baker, 2005: 21), which was built in Britain in 122 AD under the Roman Empire. At this point, scholars began to point to the historic and iconic importance of the Berlin Wall to twentieth-century history.

More importantly, a costly urban process was necessary to reunify the two parts of the city. Destruction of the territorial border was followed by the reconstruction of space – flows and entities that were physically and temporarily kept apart had to be connected again. A young generation of West and East Berliners had to create affective attachments to a city that, because of a territorial intervention, had made each part alien to the other. Iconic public spaces of the unified Berlin were rebuilt, symbolic edifices were erected and East and West Berliners retrieved indexes of an erstwhile single city. Spectacular architecture around the Mitte and Potsdamer Platz was accompanied by the 'critical reconstruction' that advocated a 'supposedly "typical" Berlin architectural tradition,' which was 'selectively appropriated and conjured as powerful visions of a traditional European city' (Colomb, 2012: 210). Roughly a decade after its demolition, public hearings were held to mark the memory of the wall, which (although physically absent) became an 'urban icon' (Schlör, 2006: 95) – or, as Brian Ladd (1997: 7) provocatively states, 'probably the most famous structure that will ever stand in Berlin.'

The architect Lebbeus Woods (2004: 24) was not invited to be part of an exhibition organized in Berlin in 1990, but nevertheless decided

Conceiving the city: what is next? 137

to propose a provocative project himself. Woods condemned the idea that, just as both East and West Germany had used the wall to enforce their respective artificial identities, unification should also use the vacant space left by the wall as a symbolic element highlighting the existing frictions that soon arose after the fall. 'The gaps are being closed, the cracks plastered over. Where will the artists, impoverished as ever, go? The renegades?' Woods saw an urban cleansing. He suggested an architectural structure, a machine-like building creating a space open to ambiguous and non-controlled uses, 'constructed secretly and outside the limits of existing building laws'. Incorporating emerging telecommunication technologies, Woods proposed a ' "free zone", a city within a city'. The Berlin Wall is inherently a territorial device, but also symbolizes the centrality of the city within the global geopolitical space, and the complexity that engenders the construction of places within a divided city.

Airports, the utmost place

In a book that became a cornerstone of contemporary discussions about place, Marc Augé gives the airport as an example of *non-place*. Non-places were defined as portions of space without historical or identity concerns, 'a world where people are born in the clinic and die in the hospital, where transit points and temporary abodes are proliferating under luxurious or inhuman conditions (. . .) where a dense network of means of transport which are also inhabited spaces is developing' (Augé, 1995: 78). Within this logic of non-place as spaces without deep-seated meaning, airports serve solely as part of a logistic infrastructure, like highways and railroads. Apart from the daily life of the cities where they are located, the spatial qualities of airports are as artificial as those of shopping malls. Still according to this logic, airports are residual spaces of global capitalism and consumerist culture.

Quite to the contrary, I argue that airports are the quintessential space in a global and interconnected world. This is not only because of their logistic aspects, but rather because of their cultural aspects, which are reflected in what they represent for the concepts of space, place and territories.

Cargo traffic helps us partially understand the geography of the global economy. In 2004, four airports in the United States were among the busiest cargo airports worldwide, followed by Asia with four, and Europe with two. Ten years later, Asia had five of the ten busiest cargo airports, followed by the United States with three. Europe had only one, and Dubai entered the list (ACI, 2005; ACI 2014). However, this is only a partial picture of global infrastructure.

138 *Conceiving the city: what is next?*

Indeed, hundreds of millions of people use airports every year. In 2015, 3.5 billion passengers flew all over the world, and the International Air Transport Association (IATA, 2015) predicts this number will double in 20 years. China, the United States, Indonesia and Brazil will lead this growth. For the same year of 2015, including domestic and international flights by carriers registered in each country, the United States led with 702 million passengers, followed by China (390 million) and the United Kingdom (125 million) (World Bank, n.d.). More than these numbers, geographic diversity can be seen by comparing 2015 with 2000, the year before the terrorist attacks against the United States using airplanes as weapons that hit the Pentagon and eradicated the World Trade Center. In 2000, the busiest airport was Atlanta with 80 million passengers, followed by Chicago (72 million), and Los Angeles (66 million). In 2015, Atlanta remained the busiest airport in the world, totalling 101 million passengers, followed by Beijing (90 million) and Dubai (78 million). In 2000, there were eighteen US airports among the thirty busiest in the world, and twelve in 2015. Finally, Tokyo was the only Asian airport among the ten busiest airports in 2000 – Europe had four, and the United States five. In 2015, there were three Asian airports, and Dubai represented the Gulf States as the third busiest (ACI, 2015; ACI, 2001).

These changes in the ranking of the busiest passenger airports reflect both a shift in the global economy towards the east, as well as changes in flight management and the airlines' business model, which has been shifting from point-to-point traffic to hub-and-spoke. Long-haul flights serve a small number of hubs, where passengers are distributed to smaller airports through shorter flights. Applying methods of network analysis for the 687 most connected airports in the world, Derudder, Devrient, and Witlox (2007) demonstrate that the hub-and-spoke model makes passengers fly to airports they do not intend to go to. For instance, for Paris-Seattle flights for the period January–August 2001, 6,000 passengers took direct flights, while another 26,000 had to take connecting flights, 7,000 of these stopping in London.

The spatial relation airports have with the site where they are located is not negligible, ranging from geographic to economic aspects. Dubai is the only airport that ranks in the top ten for both cargo and passenger traffic. And although the United Arab Emirates was also impacted by the global economic recession of 2008–2010, its airports experienced an average 75 per cent increase in passenger traffic from 2007 to 2012: notably, Dubai was not the fastest growing, but rather Abu Dhabi (112 per cent), Ras Alkhaimah (96 per cent), and Sharjah (74 per cent) were far ahead (Al Kaabi, 2015). Most of these cities rely on the Export Processing Zone (EPZ), an economic and administrative instrument used to attract foreign investments with low taxes, free ports, incentives for

Conceiving the city: what is next? 139

global companies and flexible labour legislation, 'mixing ecstatic expressions of urbanity with a complex and sometimes violent form of lawlessness' (Easterling, 2014: 26).

Besides the global economic and locational factors that determine the topological position of airports as hubs and nodes in global networks, there are the spatial determinants related to their geographic positioning. Airports 'require 360° electronic surveillance of the skies' (Edwards, 2005: 39), an operational fact that has architectural influences – airports are massive edifices often located in flat and empty fields. Access to airports requires transportation infrastructure that also has huge impacts on vast landscapes, whether expressways or parking structures, and railways and subways linking the airport to the closest city. Land use integration is also delicate. Beyond the large areas kept open for safety, warehouses and industries occupy the majority of the land, followed by business centres, conference venues and hotels. Because airports are major employers (58,000 work at Heathrow, 42,000 in Frankfurt, e.g.,), diversified urban areas with housing, commerce and public facilities are frequently attracted to the edges of airport zones. Finally, airports have significant environmental impacts, ranging from noise pollution to negative consequences for air and water quality: burning fossil fuels and groundwater contamination through fuel spillage are main concerns. The locational relationships airports establish with the regions that receive them demonstrate the spatial and territorial challenges they bring to urban and regional planning and design; these challenges cannot be easily encapsulated into the single concept of *non-place*.

And then there are the spatial complexities of the airport edifice. The airport terminal stands between two highly specialized functional zones: urban and regional infrastructures on the one side, and the runways, taxiways, hangars, control tower and warehouses on the other. Inside the terminal, functionality also prevails, and is organized around four main zones: ticketing and check-in, security and immigration checks, the departure concourse, and baggage claim. The first and fourth zones connect the airport to the outside. Security and immigration checks and the departure concourse are at the centre of the passenger's experience while at the airport.

Security and immigration checks are a burden to all passengers which became even stricter after the 2001 terrorist attacks in the United States. But this burden varies according to the passenger's citizenship when arriving at different countries. Queues created according to visa requirements are a concrete representation of global geopolitics at immigration checks, and frequent flyers with their special lines and fast tracks demonstrate another layer of citizenship. The security and immigration areas are prime sites for 'operational and legal abstractions'

140   Conceiving the city: what is next?

(Pascoe, 2001: 9), where the complex and discrete layers of control of global society are experienced. The remarkable case of Merhan Karimi Nasseri, an Iranian-born refugee who became stateless in 1981 and later spent 11 years in the basement of Charles de Gaulle Airport in Paris because he could neither enter the country nor be deported, highlights the territorial complexities that are entrenched in airports.

Finally, airports have acquired iconic and symbolic values. The crowds that used to visit airports in the 1950s and 1960s to watch landings and takeoffs still appear today in cities receiving their first airports or long-haul flights. Airports were, and remain, icons of modernity. The first plane-spotters witnessed the construction of a global space, where different time zones, languages, currencies, legal status of people and products, and cultures are constantly transacted. Airplanes and airports were indexes (signs) of this global space. New York Trans World Flight Center (now JFK), designed by Eero Saarinen in 1962, and Paris Charles de Gaulle, designed by Paul Andreu in 1965, are considered the first edifices designed to express the particular features of the modern airport. Since then, building on the airport's iconic power, cities and countries use them as symbols – either expressing nationalistic pride and an 'Olympian ideal' (Easterling, 2004: 28) or in an attempt to use landscape, architecture, interior design and art to express local cultures. Design guides for airports (e.g., Thomas-Emberson, 2007) highlight the use of local materials and aesthetic culture to create a 'sense of place' to be admired by passengers and the local population alike.

Attempts to contextualize airport buildings within the local architecture of the regions where they are situated are valid exercises. However, this approach risks making airports look even more artificial, like an architectural caricature. Witold Rybczynski (1992) confessed he has frequently been dispirited by the inactivity and ennui that characterize airports, reflected in the faces and attitudes of passengers waiting for their connecting flights. He praises Amsterdam's airport for its 'domesticity', an unexpected attribute for an airport, in contrast with the fantasy and excesses often found in international hubs. This 'domesticity' would disturb Andy Warhol (1975: 160), who, although he did not like to fly, considered airplanes and airports to have his favourite kind of food, favourite bathrooms, entertainment, graphic and colours, 'favorite loudspeaker address systems, my favorite conveyor belts'.

Airports become places not because of a pretentious aesthetic similitude with 'local architecture' (whatever this may mean). Locals do not visit airports, and most passengers do not visit the cities; when they do, either they are business people going from the airport to the hotel and meeting venues and then back to the airport, not caring about the possible local architecture, or they are tourists that perceive the

Conceiving the city: what is next? 141

artificiality of the 'local culture' inflicted upon the airport building. Airports become places for those who actually use air travel, and for them the feeling of domesticity is a relief. And domesticity, and the sense of being in one's own place and feeling at home, depends on the sensorial and cultural filters, the entities and flows that are dealt with in a portion of space. Frequent airport users are living within a global space composed of different time zones, layers of territorial legislations, languages and currencies: different entities and flows. Dealing with these elements, emphasizing some of them, and soothing others, is what turns an airport into a place: a special kind of place, to be sure, but a place for those who project their social and cultural values onto a portion of space, nonetheless.

Everywhere, anywhere, nowhere, here

In 1958, United States President Dwight D. Eisenhower sent greetings across the world via shortwave radio, using the first communication satellite. Telecommunications were about to change the world, and cities as well. Marshall McLuhan (1965) was a key theorist of media studies at the time, and heavily responsible for promoting the idea that communication media and computation would reshape our social relations, politics and space. Within McLuhan's logic, we realized that space would change drastically, and the very idea of a global space would be a concrete daily experience. Still unknown entities and flows would take the foreground in the world, and our sensorial and cultural filters would be transformed by telecommunications and computation. Consequently, new spatialities would emerge, and this new space would be everywhere.

Imbued with similar ideas, architects and designers began to pose a critical question: how would these new entities and flows be reflected in the physicality of the cities? An architectural structure embracing the whole world would be an obvious and naïve idea. In this global world, cities would still be located in specific sites, but why should architecture be static? If the new urban space, with its backbone infrastructures formed by telecommunication and computation technologies, would be everywhere, architecture could be a tool encouraging this global space to emerge anywhere.

Archigram, a group formed by British architects in the 1960s, proposed aerial cities that could be attached to any existing city. From the smallest scale of a living pod to large ephemeral urban interventions, David Greene, Peter Cook (both members of Archigram), Coop Himmelb(l)au and Haus-Rucker-Co proposed cities as 'a media event for the enjoyment of the general public' (Alison et al., 2002) – an eventful urbanity

142 *Conceiving the city: what is next?*

that could move anywhere. Peter Cook (1970: 11), responsible for the theoretical background of such experimental architecture, stated: 'any experiment that goes beyond mere technical investigation may incorporate motives that are potentially more dynamic than the physical result.' And Cook completed his reasoning of an architecture aware of emerging globalization built upon the transportation and communication technologies, saying that 'a generation of architects is growing up that is less interested in the local architecture or any region than in the pursuit of a certain attitude, from whatever part of the world it stems' (Cook, 1970: 14). At the Massachusetts Institute of Technology (MIT), Nicholas Negroponte (1975) tested responsive environments in which computers would have the potential to enhance buildings, responding not only to external conditions but changing 'states of policy', using complex algorithms that would learn from user tastes and behaviours.

The architectural euphoria of the 1960s and 1970s with telecommunications and computation technologies reshaping urban space partially faded away in the 1980s and early 1990s. In the early 1990s the Internet became commercial. At this time, Paul Virilio (1997: 13) already pointed out that urbanists would have to deal with 'the permanent requirements of organizing and constructing real space', on the one hand, and 'the new requirements of managing the real time of immediacy and ubiquity, with its access protocols, its "data packet transmissions" and its viruses', on the other hand. Virilio frequently stressed that failures and accidents were an intrinsic part of technological development, a facet he thought was hidden under the propaganda of progress. As for media such as TV, the Internet and mobile phones, Virilio 2002: 41) saw in them 'simulators of proximity' used to disguise individual incompleteness, and 'an imposture of immediacy that is more dystopian than ever'.

In this same period, while some philosophers saw the consequences of the pervasiveness of information and communication technologies as producing 'collective intelligence' where knowledge would be created through sometimes unexpected dialogues and exchanges of ideas on a global scale (Lévy, 1997), others only saw extreme individualization, with individuals focused on personal interests and only communicating with themselves through computers, as cocoons. Also at this time, authors used Marc Augé's (1995) concept of non-places to analyze spaces that were connected to other distant similar spaces through telecommunication technologies, but were not related to their own neighbouring and heterogeneous spaces. For some time, it seemed that space had no future – as predicted by Frances Cairncross (1997: 2), when she said, 'The death of distance and the communications revolution will be among the most important forces shaping economies and society in the next fifty years or

Conceiving the city: what is next? 143

so.' The future of space was nowhere. These bleak ideas were balanced with enthusiastic views of how information technologies were already changing our lives by combining 'the comprehensive geographic coverage and sophisticated person-to-person and place-to-place connection capabilities' (Mitchell, 1999: 14). William Mitchell was behind the creation of the Media Laboratory at MIT, which would become a power plant for new experiments on the verge of the physicality of buildings and the increasing implementation of sensors and data streams which had already started to pervade social life.

A decade after dystopian euphoria surrounding the end of space, balanced by growing research on how pervasive information technologies would deeply reshape our daily lives and spaces, a millennial common sense idea began to be expressed as a deep insight: place matters. True, information and communication technologies created a global space where data flows relatively freely, and pervasive sensors collect all sorts of data about the natural environment, buildings and infrastructure, biometrics and physiological features and functionalities of individuals, and all sorts of social and financial interactions. By the end of the 1990s, Mitchell (1999: 14) had already proclaimed that

> everyday objects – from wristwatches to wallboard – will become smarter and smarter, and will serve as our interfaces to the ubiquitous digital world. And paradoxically, wherever you happen to come in contact with this immense collective construction, it will seem to have the intimacy of underwear.

In this context, Mitchell (2003) echoed a lingering idea between media scholars that in the information era and its pervasive wireless digital technologies, buildings and cities need less specialized spaces, and might be functionally, aesthetically, and socially reconfigured, serving multiple purposes. A café becomes an office, a trip on the subway a movie session, and a living room becomes all of the above, in an endless array of unanticipated uses, designed not through the arrangement of objects and assigned functions, but through the relations established between dwellers' moods and behaviours (tracked through sensors), digital devices and once inanimate objects now embedded with smart materials and communication technologies.

Still, place matters, not only because it is where social friction and traction take place, but because of the opposite notion: it is where social friction and traction exist that places emerge. Places are formed where personal or social values are shared and are reflected onto a portion of space. This is why an airport is also a place, not simply a node; this is also why the same portion of space may become multiple and

144 *Conceiving the city: what is next?*

unanticipated places, not restricted by functionalities initially assigned by architects. So if information and communication technologies instil possibilities for creating a global space that would be everywhere, we are at the point where the power to create such global spaces lies here. And here. And here.

On the one hand, as technology companies are the lead stakeholders investing in parts of the city to increase the capability of their information and communication infrastructures in order to attract innovative companies (quite often benefitting from public funds), there is the risk that 'the oligopolistic character of the tech industry might result in smart cities that are mute to one another' (Van Timmeren and Henriquez, 2015: 93). On the other hand, there is the emergence of a network of locations that try to connect with each other and at the same time attempt to reinforce their uniqueness as places. They actually market their place-ness as an asset to attract companies and businesspeople that transit in global spaces.

What emerges from the infiltration of information and communication technologies into physical spaces and social and economic spheres can be experienced on different levels. Cities are promoting specific areas as their prime digital or innovation districts, while at the same time the coexistence of physical and digital features of urbanity opens up possibilities for unexpected spatial and social organizations, as well as epistemological challenges to fully understand contemporary urban realities.

An example of an innovation district is 22@BCN in Barcelona, Spain (Barcelona, 2000). Like many cities around the world, Barcelona experienced a period of growing deindustrialization that left 200 hectares of former industrial land in the heart of the city. In 2000, the city launched the project with two goals: to make Barcelona a leading centre for scientific and technological production in the knowledge economy, and to promote the integration and functional reconversion of a traditional industrial neighbourhood located near the downtown area. Underlying this second goal was harsh criticism the city received after urban interventions in the late 1980s in preparation for the Olympics. The first goal echoes claims of the importance of 'creative' industries in reigniting local economies (Florida, 2005). 22@BCN attracted high-tech industries in five areas: media, information and communication technologies (ICTs), medical technology, energy and design. Buildings were leased to research universities, high-end housing and commercial buildings were erected, and parks and boulevards were built to attract new residents.

22@BCN was also intended to promote integration with Poblenou, the old industrial neighbourhood. In the 1990s, this area was occupied by housing blocs that did not comply with Cerdà's masterplan, and tens of hectares of unused industrial land containing beautifully crafted factories with significant historical value – when the 22@BCN plan was approved in 2000, forty-six industrial buildings were listed as industrial heritage (Duarte, Sabaté, 2013). When the urban interventions began, residents were stunned by the demolition of some of this industrial heritage, which seemed to indicate a deep disregard for the community. Almost 20 years after its conception, 22@BCN is still the testing ground for new urban technologies and an important economic engine in the knowledge economy, but also fertile terrain for understanding the struggles between an entrenched local culture and the power of the global economy based on information and communication technologies.

Pervasive technologies change experiences of urbanity. We have incorporated entities and flows into our daily lives that barely 10 years ago had not even been imagined, or were limited to research centres. As we incorporate these entities and flows as part of our cultural values, and as they change our sensorial perception of space and time, places within the global networks of information and communication technologies continue to be portions of space where we reflect and share personal and social values, places that today are constituted by malleable mixings of temporal and geographic scales. But still places that prove to be the repository of personal and cultural values, and become a safe point in turbulent times. But also places that create tractions and frictions that propel the creation of new spatialities.

References

ACI (2001) Passenger Traffic 2000 FINAL. Airports Council International. At www.aci.aero/Data-Centre/Annual-Traffic-Data/Passengers/2000-final

ACI (2005) Cargo Traffic 2004 FINAL. Airports Council International. At www.aci.aero/Data-Centre/Annual-Traffic-Data/Cargo/2004-final

ACI (2014) Cargo Traffic 2013 FINAL. Airports Council International. At www.aci.aero/Data-Centre/Annual-Traffic-Data/Cargo/2013-final

ACI (2015) Year to date Passenger Traffic. Airports Council International. At www.aci.aero/Data-Centre/Monthly-Traffic-Data/Passenger-Summary/Year-to-date

Al Kaabi, Khaula; Abdulla, Saif (2015) "The air transport system of United Arab Emirates during the global financial crisis and Arab spring". In: Conventz, Sven; Thierstein, Alain (eds) *Airports, cities and regions*. London: Routledge, 47–67.

Alison, Jane; Brayer, Marie-Ange; Migayrou, Frédéric; Spiller Neil (2002) *Future city: Experiment and utopia in architecture*. New York, NY: Thames & Hudson.

Augé, Marc (1995) *Non-Places. Introduction to an anthropology of super-modernity*. London: Verso.

Aureli, Pier Vittorio (2011) *The possibility of an absolute architecture*. Cambridge, MA: MIT Press.

146 *Conceiving the city: what is next?*

Baker, Frederik (2005) "The Berlin Wall". In: Ganster, Paul; Lorey, David (eds) *Borders and border politics in a globalizing world.* Oxford: SR Books, 21–49.

Cairncross, Frances (1997) *The death of distance: How the communications revolution is changing our lives.* Cambridge, MA: Harvard Business School Press.

Colomb, Clare (2012) *Staging the new Berlin. Place marketing and the politics of urban reinvention post-1989.* London: Routledge.

Cook, Peter (1970) *Experimental architecture.* New York, NY: Universe Books.

Derudder, Ben; Devrient, Lomme; Witlox, Frank (2007) Flying where you don't want to go: An empirical analysis of hubs in the global airline network. *Tijdschrift voor Economische en Sociale Geografie [Journal of Economic & Social Geography],* 98(3): 307–324.

Duarte, Fábio; Sabaté, Joaquín (2013) 22@Barcelona: Creative economy and industrial heritage – a critical perspective. *Theoretical and Empirical Researches in Urban Management,* 8(2): 5–21.

Easterling, Keller (2014). *Extrastatecraft. The power of infrastructure space.* London: Verso.

Edwards, Brian (2005) *The modern airport terminal. New approaches to airport architecture* (2nd edition) London: Spon.

Florida, Richard (2005) *Cities and the creative class.* New York, NY: Routledge.

Gravel, Ryan (2016) *Where we want to live. Reclaiming infrastructure for a new generation of cities.* New York, NY: St. Martin's Press.

Hays, Michael (2010) *Architecture's desire. Reading the late avant-garde.* Cambridge, MA: MIT Press.

Hess Alan (1993) *Viva Las Vegas: After-Hours architecture.* San Francisco, CA: Chronicle Books.

Hillier, Bill; Laura, Vaughan (2007) The city as one thing. *Progress in planning,* 67(3): 205–230.

IATA (2015) "IATA Air Passenger Forecast Shows Dip in Long-Term Demand". *IATA Press Release 55,* November 26. At www.iata.org/pressroom/pr/Pages/ 2015-11-26-01.aspx

Koolhaas, Rem (1994) *Delirious New York.* New York, NY: Monacelli.

Ladd, Brian (1997) *The ghosts of Berlin: Confronting German history in the Urban landscape.* Chicago, IL: University of Chicago Press.

Lefebvre, Henri (2014) *Towards an architecture of enjoyment.* Minneapolis, MN: University of Minnesota Press (© 1973).

Lévy, Pierre (1997) *L'intelligence collective: Pour une anthropologie du cyberspace.* Paris: La Découverte.

McLuhan, Marshall (1965) *Understanding media: the extensions of man.* New York, NY: McGraw-Hill.

Mercier, Pascal (2008) *Night train to Lisbon.* New York, NY: Grove Press.

Mitchell, William (1996) *City of bits: space, place, and the infobahn.* Cambridge, MA: MIT Press.

Mitchell, William (1999) *e-topia.* Cambridge, MA: MIT Press.

Mitchell, William (2003) *Me++. The cyborg self and the networked city.* Cambridge, MA: MIT Press.

Negroponte, Nicholas (1975) *Soft architecture machines.* Cambridge, MA: MIT Press.

Pascoe, David (2001) *Airspaces.* London: Reaktion.

Pugh, Emily (2014) *Architecture, politics, & identity in divided Berlin*. Pittsburgh: University of Pittsburgh Press.

Rybczynski, Witold (1992) *Looking around*. New York, NY: Viking.

Stanek, Lukasz (2011) *Henri Lefebvre on space. Architecture, urban research, and the production of theory*. Minneapolis: University of Minnesota Press.

Schlör, Joachim (2006) 'It has to go away, but at the same time it has to be kept': The Berlin Wall and the making of an urban icon. *Urban History*, 33(1): 85–105.

Steinberg, Ted (2014) *Gotham unbound: The ecological history of greater New York*. New York, NY: Simon & Schuster.

Thomas-Emberson, Steve (2007) *Airport interiors. Design for business*. London: Wiley.

Van Timmeren, Arjan; Henriquez, Laurence (2015) *Ubikquity & the illuminated city*. Delft: TU-Delft.

Virilio, Paul (1997) *Open sky*. London: Verso. Translated by Julie Rose, of *La Vitesse de Libération* (1995).

Virilio, Paul (2002) *Ground zero*. London: Verso (Translated by Chris Turner, of *Ce qui arrive*).

Wahrol, Andy (1975) "Atmosphere". In: *The Philosophy of Andy Warhol: From A to B and Back Again*. Orlando, FL: Harcourt, 139–160.

Waldheim, Charles (2016) *Landscape urbanism*. New York: Princeton University Press.

Woods, Lebbeus (2004) *Experimental architecture*. Pittsburgh: Carnegie Museum of Art.

World Bank (n.d.) "Air transport, passengers carried" – World Bank Data. At: http://data.worldbank.org/indicator/IS.AIR.PSGR

8   Challenging the city

We get used to space, and get used to the entities and flows that have been selected to compose the space we live in. We get used to the way these entities and flows are organized. Any unexpected entities and flows that enter the space, or any disruptions in the spatial arrangement we are used to, create imbalances in our spatial matrix – the way we perceive and understand space. Spatial arrangements change, true. And they change both with the entrance of new elements onto the scene as well as with the re-emergence of obliterated elements. The appearance of motorized vehicles was disruptive for cities: they introduced speeds that were unknown to city life, they changed the way other entities and flows had to be organized and relate to each other. Roads were widened, and the street grid was rectified to accommodate motor vehicles. Likewise, public lighting has definitively transformed urban space. For one thing, it added time to public life in the streets and changed social life. Today, when blackouts occur, they do not remind us that once cities were dark after dusk. Instead of pointing to the fact that artificial lighting is a relatively new urban entity, blackouts seem to introduce a new entity to the urban space: darkness. Both new elements and the re-emergence of obliterated elements challenge the way we deal with urban spaces. However, changes in the urban space tend to occur slowly and are accompanied by social transformations (the introduction of motorized vehicles or public lighting) or are the temporary results of failures (blackouts).

In the previous chapter I discussed architectural and urban interventions that propose new spatialities: how to organize entities and flows considering the emergence of new elements in the urban space. These proposals challenge our perception and understanding of space. But they are committed to changing space in the long term, sometimes pushing for a deterministic view. One example is Rem Koolhaas's claim that late-nineteenth-century innovations such as elevators or air conditioning have not entered architectural thinking yet, only as mere additions to traditional ways of conceiving space which still prevail.

150 *Challenging the city*

Charles Jencks (Jencks, Koolhaas, 2014) contests Koolhaas's argument as technological fatalism:

> *Koolhaas*: But the ideology and inner core of architecture has been incredibly resistant to the understanding that, since 1850, things have fundamentally changed. (. . .) the effects of the mechanical devices were not incorporated into architectural thinking, the effects on the morphology of the skyscraper and the cities. (. . .) We had architecture and then we had the mechanical systems – not that 'architecture is now these mechanisms'.

> *Jencks*: There is, of course, the problem of technical determinism in your position like Choisy or Banham or Bucky Fuller's evolution. But we know the problem with technological fatalism is that it does not engage with a lot of things, such as social changes in the larger sphere; how people are living today is more important than 'smart walls'.

Another example of defying the status quo as a means of paving the way to a different idea came when Peter Eisenman (Jencks, Eisenman, 1989: 50), also in an interview with Charles Jencks, claimed he placed columns in the middle of a bedroom, making it impossible to fit a bed inside, as a way of questioning the 'symbolism of function', the meaning impregnated in this spatial arrangement (bedroom). The function (a bedroom is made for sleeping in a bed) is considered as an ingrained meaning that is not inalienable from the entities and flows that form this portion of space. Radical, candid or wrecked, such arguments aim to challenge the way of considering space, but they also have a purpose: they propose the way we should think of space – what, ultimately, undermines the extent of the challenge as an investigative procedure *per se*.

This is what interests me in this chapter: actions that challenge space but do not aim to replace one thing with another; spatial challenges that are intended to unbalance the way we perceive and understand space for the sake of making us uncomfortable with stabilized spatial rationales. The token they offer is not a better or smarter space, but the libertarian feeling of probing our beliefs in what is supposed to be urban space. For this reason, I focus on temporary projects varying from large regional-scale artistic interventions to anonymous actions that do not leave any trace on the city, not even temporary traces, but challenge the restrictive and over-ruled way we look at the city.

In 1983, the artist Christo and Jeanne-Claude surrounded eleven islands in Biscayne Bay, in Miami, Florida, with 6.5 million square feet of pink polypropylene fabric. It was impressive. It was beautiful. It was challenging. Islands still have an aura of untouched spaces, of a lifestyle

Figure 8.1 Christo and Jeanne-Claude, *Surrounded Islands*, 1980–83 © Photo: Wolfgang Volz

152   Challenging the city

detached from busy urban areas. The pink fabric of *Surrounded Islands* seemed so out of place because this artwork challenged the sense of normality – and moreover, the intervention was stunning, attracting thousands of people. It raised several questions: why would surrounding islands with pink fabric seem any more aggressive to the spatial organization of Biscayne Bay than boats and yachts? Why would Christo's and and Jeanne-Claude's 2-week artistic action raise more environmental concerns, and go through a longer approval process, than the buildings built next to the ocean, permanently changing the character of the coast?

Surrounded Islands is part of a series of wrapping interventions Christo started when he moved to Paris in the 1950s, a stop on his journey from Bulgaria to the United States. By wrapping objects, Christo made sculptures out of ordinary materials. Instead of carving stone or assembling pieces, the artist added a layer of fabric to envelop objects, and by adding this element he revealed some features of these objects that usually pass unnoticed, revealing the blindness that comes with habit.

In Paris he met Jeanne-Claude, who became his wife and partner. At that point, Jeanne-Claude was not an artist in the usual sense of the word. Christo and Jeanne-Claude have always emphasized that their creative process could not be understood only in terms of what one could call artistic inspiration and talent, but also involved site selection, negotiations with different stakeholders and long fundraising campaigns. These are all aspects that are part of many architectural and urban projects, but usually remain in the background. As Matthias Koddenberg (2015: 19) observes, during their years in Paris, Christo and Jeanne-Claude 'took in whatever the town spat out as a result of its unbridled hunger and constant change'. Jeanne-Claude was fully engaged in all aspects of the construction of space, which involves the selection and arrangement of entities and flows other than the visible ones. As C. Thomas Mitchell (1993: 107) states, 'the physical artifact is a part, but only a transitory part, of the art experience.'

Christo's charcoal and pastel sketches and collages of the initial ideas as well as the final technical drawings of his interventions had to be sold to raise money to implement the projects, which are funded entirely by the artist. Christo's and Jeanne-Claude's projects take years from initial conception to final construction, a process that also involves several public hearings with the local population in the affected areas and multiple committees, meetings with public officials, approval of environmental impact assessments – activities that other artists, architects and designers seldom let the public see. Burt Chernow (2002: 240), who followed the career of Christo and Jeanne-Claude for decades and wrote a biography of the couple, narrates this process for installing *Running Fence* (1972–1976), a 24½-mile fence made of 18-foot high white nylon fabric and 2,050 steel poles that crossed private ranches, roads and towns in California:

> The vote [in the Marin County Planning Commission] was four to one for granting the use permit. However, only about four of the fence's twenty-four and a half miles were regulated by Marin County; Christo and Jeanne-Claude still needed approval from Sonoma County, the Coastal Commission, the State Lands Commission, and the Army Corps of Engineers. He expressed relief at the decision, hoping it would set the tone for forthcoming hearings.

As Christo has stated,

> Running Fence is not the poles, it's not the canvas or the cables; but the hills, the ocean, the land, the farms, the farmers, the roads, the landscape, the people and their relationships, I mean, there's an invisible part of Running Fence which is lived by a large part of the population, in the community where the project is rooted, where it is growing up.
>
> (*apud* Mitchell, 1993: 106)

It took 10 years for Christo and Jeanne-Claude to receive permission to wrap the Pont-Neuf in Paris. Finally, in 1985 about 300 workers completed this 2-week intervention, using 400,000 square feet of sandstone-coloured woven polyamide fabric and 12 tons of steel chains encircling the towers of the bridge 3 feet under the Seine. Dominique Laporte (1986: 21) sees the 'reverse of sacrifice' in Christo's and Jeanne-Claude's wrapping the stone, turning the bridge into a phantom. Christo and Jeanne-Claude reveal the functions and symbolisms of architectural monuments by covering them, by making them temporarily invisible. And people's resistance to Christo's and Jeanne-Claude's interventions shows 'an irrational fear (...) a dim presentiment of menace which seems to compel a resistance to this exceedingly simple and singularly gentle endeavor' (Laporte, 1986: 19).

Arguably Christo's and Jeanne-Claude's most political intervention is the wrapping of the Reichstag, the German parliament in Berlin. Wrapping a national parliament is in itself a bold and brave act. Wrapping the Reichstag ended a 24-year project, from the first sketches to the public hearings and its execution in 1995. The nineteenth-century building was severely damaged by a fire in 1933, was almost completely destroyed in 1945, and was restored in the 1960s – but always remained a symbol of German unity, which it would recover with the post-1989 reunification.

154 *Challenging the city*

Final approval of Christo's and Jeanne-Claude's project came with a plenary session in 1994, which was televised live and passed with 57 per cent of the valid votes. The *Wrapped Reichstag* received more than five million visitors (Chernow, 2002).

Christo and Jeanne-Claude challenge the comfortable and often uncritical relationships we establish with space. We get used to drastic, damaging, and lasting urban interventions, from omnipresent cars taking over livable and communal space to the artificial nature of Dubai's islands, full of cheap symbolism, while gentle and temporary artistic interventions like Christo's and Jeanne-Claude's installations still raise social, aesthetic and environmental concerns. Christo's and Jeanne-Claude's works add a mix of the fear we feel with the introduction of unexpected elements to space, or the sudden abduction of familiar urban elements. When he extended 24 miles of fabric through the California landscape, the act reminded us of all the other interventions that permanently disrupted the landscape; when he wrapped a stone bridge in Paris, it was as if he seized an intrinsic element of the Parisian urban space. In both situations, Christo and Jeanne-Claude challenge our perception of space by proposing a landscape that should not exist.

The arrangement of entities and flows that constitute urban spaces tends to stabilize. Even the unstoppable movement of people and bicycles, cars, buses and trucks, subways and trains, which gives the impression of a rootless space, is actually static when seen within a longer-time perspective. These moving parts of the city repeat their movement every day, going through the same locations at the same time. This stability yields security: we know how to move through space, we know how to deal with certain entities and flows, we know what to expect from space, and what space expects from us. This stabilization creates rules. True, rules are essentially a territorial characteristic. But space also has rules, which are so deeply ingrained in the way we deal with entities and flows that we do not realize these rules do not belong to these elements, but rather have been added to them. For instance, the way people behave in the streets has been highly regulated, mostly for pedestrians' own safety: if you walk in the street as if you were in an open field, changing directions at will and stopping abruptly to observe what catches your attention, you will probably get hit. Therefore, the implicit message is that it is better to respect regulations imposed upon spatial elements. Although traffic regulations are substantially similar all over the world, the way people behave in relation to them varies significantly between countries and even between cities. Seen from a distance, motorized vehicles, pedestrians, and bicycles, sidewalks and roadways with similar dimensions and design comprise the road space in Mumbai, London and Sydney. But how people deal with these elements, how they interact with each other, varies considerably. In terms of safety, I would walk almost blindly in Sydney, while quite a few times I instinctively grabbed the arm of a colleague to cross streets in Mumbai. Cultural filters not only select which entities and flows constitute our space, but how we deal with these elements as well.

Regardless of my feelings as a pedestrian in these three cities, they all have traffic rules which often give preference to motorized vehicles, despite recent efforts to implement bike paths, the extension and width of roads, and traffic light cycles indicating which mode of transportation has right of way. Comparing photographs of the early-twentieth-century metropolis, cars, streetcars, horses and pedestrians had to negotiate space with each other: who could occupy which portion for how long. Rules slowly became an invisible constituent of space. It is not that a territory has already been established, but that rules became another spatial element. In this process, space has been stabilized – until other entities and flows are incorporated or challenge this stability.

As Shelley Smith (2010: 148) points out, when we become unable 'to influence our physical environment, we are stripped of responsibility and become alienated'. Artists question the stability of urban spaces, and their work is important to show us how accustomed we have become to spatial rules, but also how restrictive such rules are. Likewise, architects and urban designers also try to challenge such spatial rules, as we have discussed in previous chapters. However, it is equally or even more intriguing when ordinary people challenge these spatial rules, or the functions and meanings attributed to spatial elements. Benches are designed for sitting, sidewalks for pedestrians, walls and fences to separate areas, and handrails for protection and guidance. *Traceurs* (loosely but commonly translated as free runners) challenge these functions and meanings. They take urban entities for their concrete values: a staircase is not an architectural element designed to join areas on different levels by combining horizontal and vertical planes with dimensions comfortable enough to be surmounted by a walking person. From this phrase, *traceurs* would only pay attention to 'element combining horizontal and vertical planes'. The function, the rule and the meaning of the object do not matter. And this intentional lack of established meaning and function opens up multiple possibilities. The value of the element combining horizontal and vertical planes will arise from its physical characteristics, the body's features, the physical capabilities of the user (*traceur*) and the user's purpose, which ultimately is to explore what possible movements can be created through the interaction of two elements: the human body and the object, both destitute of their socially expected functions and behaviours.

Traceurs practice parkour, a physical training method initially created in France by the military officer Georges Hébert, got attention among the

156 *Challenging the city*

youth in the Parisian *banlieues* in the 1980s. 'Parkour turns the stasis of the built environment into flux' (Smith, 2010: 151), and *traceurs* turn bland urban structures into objects of play (Kidder, 2012). While Christo and Jeanne-Claude's interventions add unexpected and temporary entities to space, *traceurs* challenge space by changing its flows. *Traceurs* deal with spatial entities through 'relative velocities, vectors, directions and momentums'. Spatial meanings emerge only temporarily during parkour, combining the relationships that different bodies and emotions – excitement, fear, pain, joy – establish with the physical characteristics of space. Parkour deals with the 'emotional content of mobility, each and every movement (and indeed stillness) begins to gather significance' (Saville, 2008: 896).

Monuments and specific buildings have their architectural forms filled with symbolic values. Monuments can be sculptural assemblages, such as obelisks and statues, as well as buildings; these are mostly state buildings, but sometimes private buildings also embody social values. In both cases, the architectural form is filled with symbolic values. Monuments have a clear territorial role in the city. Their function is to convey a message, to ascertain that those sharing a portion of space constantly remember the symbols that encompass specific political and social values. Monuments are intended to be permanent, lasting longer than the constant transformation of entities and flows that form the city, whose arrangements and values vary with time. Space changes with social, cultural and technological changes, while monuments are there to remind society of which (supposedly) core social values should be kept, values that are the symbolic amalgam of society.

Territory is the portion of space whose entities and flows are impregnated with the values that must be followed by those living within it, and the values that must be recognized by outsiders. Territory is where shared social values tend to become rules. While boundaries safeguard the limits of this portion of space, symbols such as language and national anthems are constant reminders of the values and rules of a territory. In a similar manner, monuments are territorial devices. Their presence in the city makes them landmarks, and their physicality tends to disguise the fact that their main purpose is to be a symbol.

During social turmoil, monuments are frequently attacked. And in social uprisings monuments are pulled down, often as a symbolic act confronting the social and political values these monuments represent. The storming of the Bastille in 1789 Paris, or the fall of the Berlin Wall in 1989, and the 2015 destruction of the Baalshamin temple in Palmyra, Syria, are examples of architectural monuments targeted by social and political upheavals. These are radical territorial acts. They perpetrate the destruction of a symbol through a symbolic act: making the destruction the symbol of proposed (often imposed) new values and rules. These acts question the entities and symbols of a territory, but give as a response a new territory.

Monuments suffer smaller attacks daily, though. Graffitists have made monuments their prime target. Graffitists contest the official values conveyed by monuments by defacing them. When they vandalize monuments, graffitists show their disdain for such values. Graffitists target the quasi-sacredness that monuments have acquired within specific territorial arrangements.

True, graffiti has acquired the status of art, mostly during the 1970s in New York. It was an especially tense time in the city. Unlike the political content depicted in European graffiti at the time, exemplified by the western side of the Berlin Wall, New York's graffiti 'was all style' (Cresswell, 1996: 32). Even though the city spent 10 million dollars and arrested 1,562 people in 1972 in an attempt to halt graffiti, it became part of New York's counterculture. Yet this picture of graffiti as a grassroots art form might be misleading. In contested areas, graffitists defy imposed territorial values as much as they wield other forms of territorialities. Susan Phillips (1999: 339) states that 'gang members use graffiti to close themselves into bounded systems: they cordoned off territories, make their place within neighborhoods, define friends and enemies, and in the process negotiate a host of political and cultural concerns.' Graffiti gangs develop graphic styles that are meant to be recognized by other gangs. All of them claim to despise the values impregnated in monuments. At the same time, when they vandalize them it is less a message against such imposed social values, and more often a set of ciphered messages targeting other gangs. Therefore, it is less a matter of challenging institutionalized territorial symbols and more taking advantage of the monuments (their position, their visibility) to establish parallel territorialities.

Both the destruction of monuments as well as their use as urban canvases for inscribing territorial symbols challenge well-established territorial devices. However, this challenge is accomplished by erasing or replacing objects and symbols.

Krzysztof Wodiczko has been questioning architectural monuments and the social and cultural symbolisms they bear for decades, acting upon them while still leaving them intact as objects. Wodiczko projects still and video images onto public monuments and buildings. All of his projects explore the limits of the balance between inquisitorial provocation and a polemic social issue, with a deep respect for the personal lives of those who often give private testimonies to be used in his artwork. Wodiczko also balances general social issues with the selection of particular monuments and buildings.

158 Challenging the city

In 1988, Wodiczko proposed projecting on two consecutive nights in Tijuana, Mexico and San Diego in the United States. He used the buildings to show the repressed inheritance of the cities' Spanish past, which is still present in illegal labour and desperate immigrants trying to cross the border and go north. In 1987, he projected a person equipped for a gas attack on the tower of the Martin Luther Church in Kassel, Germany, one of the few structures to survive the bombings in World War II; only 6 months prior, the city was evacuated because of air pollution. In 1990, he disguised Lenin as a Polish shopper with a cart full of electronics, projecting this image onto a Stalinist monument in Berlin which was later demolished.

As Patricia Phillips (1993: 48) puts it, 'Wodiczko uses architecture as his accomplice.' Aware of the symbolic meaning of the buildings and monuments he chooses, aware that they were designed to convey a message, Wodiczko superimposes his projections not using the building as blank canvas, but exploring these very symbolic values. He temporarily superimposes layers of meanings over crystallized meanings in a metalinguistic action. He does not try to unmask these symbolic values by exposing them, but rather by superimposing other values – even temporarily, they challenge the symbols that became impregnated into the architecture of these buildings.

Often social problems are full of personal histories that commonly pass unnoticed under the symbolic weight of monuments, which serve the

Figure 8.2 Krzysztof Wodiczko, *Homeless Projection*, 2014 © Krzysztof Wodiczko

function of securing a certain social cohesion. Wodiczko projects such personal testimonies onto monuments and monumental buildings. Again, he superimposes meanings. For a moment, a person's history, full of nuances and hidden and painful confidences, gains relevance over the pasteurized symbols of the monuments. Wodikzko listens to each person attentively, with empathy and intimate care (Art 21, 2005). In some cases, he records their testimonies and projects them onto the buildings – often only parts of the body. In 2001 he returned to Tijuana, Mexico. This time he used a headset with a camera and a microphone mounted in the front, which filmed only the face of the person from a close-up perspective. Live testimonies of pain, violence and delusion among women employed by Tijuana's *maquiladoras* were projected onto the façade of the Centro Cultural de Tijuana[1], facing the United States across the border. In 2004, Wodiczko discussed the effects of urban violence in poignant videos projected onto the St Louis Public Library, mixing the testimonies of persons who lost family members and those of inmates at the Missouri State Correctional Facility, showing only their hands. In 2014 Wodiczko promoted a dialogue between Montreal's homeless by projecting their images onto the façade of the Théâtre Maisonneuve in that city.

Building on the philosophy of Foucault, Sanford Kwinter (2011: 8) states that Wodiczko works in a 'correlative space', and is interested in the relationships between personal experiences and social spaces that create the public domain, which is 'a world of relations, relations of matter as well as speech in a form so intermingled that it is impossible to say where speech begins and where the monument ends'.

Although his projects take place in the city, Wodiczko (1992: 93) has a scathing opinion about art in public spaces: 'To believe that the city can be affected by open-air art galleries or enriched by outdoor curatorial adventures (. . .) is to commit an ultimate philosophical and political error.' More recently, advocating for a transformative engagement of design, Wodiczko (2014: 115) said that the avant-garde aim should be 'bringing into the foreground the experience, performance and presence of those whose life, work and survival is relegated to the outside of privileged fields of vision'.

Challenging urban spaces and territories, challenging the permanence and stability of entities and flows we have gotten used to, without proposing – and promoting – a substitute, might easily slip into pure contestation. From Christo's large projects to the unexpected explorations of the physical aspects of the city by *traceurs*, to Wodiczko's ephemeral and poignant projections: what these projects have in common is that they challenge our own perception and understanding of space. They do not operate by erasure. They do not operate through replacement.

160 *Challenging the city*

They operate by challenging the stabilized urban space as much as the crystallized way we perceive and understand space. More than challenging the entities and flows that constitute space and territories, these projects challenge our sensorial and cultural filters. Experiencing these projects opens up the possibility of exploring urban spaces afresh.

Note

1. www.art21.org/images/krzysztof-wodiczko/the-tijuana-projection-2001.

References

Art 21 – Television Program (2005) "Episode: Power". PBS – Art 21. At www.pbs.org/art21/artists/krzysztof-wodiczko
Chernow, Burt (2002) *Christo and Jeanne-Claude: A biography*. New York, NY: St. Martin's Press.
Cresswell, Tim (1996) *In place, out of place*. Minneapolis, MN: University of Minnesota Press.
Jencks, Charles; Eisenman, Peter (1989) Peter Eisenman: An architectural design interview by Charles Jencks. *Architectural Design*, 59(3–4): 50.
Jencks, Charles; Koolhaas, Rem (2014). The flying dutchman: Charles Jencks interviews Rem Koolhaas on his Biennale. *The Architectural Review*, June 12. At www.architectural-review.com/archive/profiles-and-interviews/the-flying-dutchman-charles-jencks-interviews-rem-koolhaas-on-his-biennale/8664063.fullarticle
Kidder, Jeffrey (2012) Parkour, the affective appropriation of urban space, and the real/virtual dialectic. *City & Community*, 11(3): 229–253.
Koddenberg, Matthias (2015) *Christo and Jeanne-Claude: in/out studio*. Dortmund, Germany: Kettler.
Kwinter, Sanford (2011) "Introduction". In: Wodiczko, Krzysztof (ed) *Krzysztof Wodiczko*. London: Black Dog.
Laporte, Dominique (1986) *Christo*. New York, NY: Pantheon.
Mitchell, Thomas C. (1993) *Redefining designing. From form to experience*. New York, NY: Van Nostrand Reinhold.
Phillips, Patricia (1993) "Images of repression". In: Wodiczko, Krzysztof (ed) *Public Address*. Minneapolis, MN: Walker Art Center, 42–53.
Phillips, Susan (1999) *Wallbangin': Graffiti and gangs in L.A.* Chicago, IL: University of Chicago Press.
Saville, Stephen (2008) Playing with fear: Parkour and the mobility of emotion. *Social & Cultural Geography*, 9(8): 891–914.
Smith, Shelley (2010) "Discovering urban voids & vertical spaces". In: Kiib, Hans (ed) *Performative urban design*. Aalborg: Aalborg University Press.
Wodiczko, Krzysztof (1993) *Krzysztof Wodiczko: Instruments, projeccions, vehicles*. Barcelona: Fundació Antoni Tàpies.
Wodiczko, Krzysztof (2014) The transformative avant-garde. A manifest of the present. *Third Text*, 28(2): 111–122.

9 Final remarks
Spatial negotiations

At the core of this book is the idea of a spatial matrix formed by space, place and territory, and that this matrix is an intellectual tool for understanding how persons or social groups shape and are shaped by spatial features. Space is defined as the arrangement of entities (natural and man-made) and flows (material and immaterial) screened by sensorial and cultural filters. Place and territory are portions of space imbued with personal and social values. While the former is centripetal, amalgamating values projected onto a portion of space, the latter is centrifugal, with values intended to influence everyone and everything within its range.

The difference between space, place and territory lies neither in importance nor scale. Although they share the same conceptual substratum, they are simultaneously singular and complementary. This spatial matrix serves as an intellectual device that permits analysis of the complexities of spatial phenomena regardless of size: a nation can be considered a place, and different territories can exist in a single bedroom. By focusing on the arrangements of entities and flows screened by sensorial and cultural values, buildings, gravitational fields and dreams are equally important to the construction of spaces – their inclusion depends on the cultural background, context and purposes of a person or social groups.

Therefore, we might say that being in space is a continuous negotiation with entities and flows: those we are able to perceive, those we can filter in and out, and the way we arrange them. And these individual and social negotiations create multiple spaces, as well as places and territories.

Recalling an example we discussed previously, early modern cities smelled of smoke from factories, and densely populated settlements, deprived of sanitation, stank of slaughterhouses, tanneries, and animal and human remains. In contemporary western cities, which slowly have been depleted of smells, such elements have been alienated from our spatial perception. In other cultures, smells still function as identifiers of neighbourhoods and streets. Tied to specific locations, they become constituent features of these portions of space. Similar to smells, noises

162 *Final remarks: spatial negotiations*

and darkness are spatial features we deal with every day, but their importance to the perception of space and their meaning have been changing throughout history and from one culture to another. We negotiate with these entities and flows, individually and as a society, historically as well as daily. These elements do not autonomously form the spaces, places and territories we live in. What I argue in this book is that space (and consequently, places and territories) is dynamically formed by how we negotiate entities and flows, by how we select and arrange them.

Such negotiations happen through the senses, intellect and culture – and each influences the other. The Inuit perceive a range a whiteness most of us living in cities do not perceive; we interact with entities and flows through man-made devices that broaden our spatial perception which are unconceivable by peoples living in regions untouched by modern civilization. We understand outer space, and how it influences our existence, in a way our forebears two generations ago could not imagine, and yet at the same time the Mayas founded their cities centuries ago based on constellations, using complex spatial logics we are still deciphering.

Spatial negotiations rely on sensorial and cultural filters that influence each other. Identifying that the perception, understanding and appropriation of space, place and territory depends on how we negotiate with entities and flows, makes them malleable concepts. Not in the sense that their conceptual definition changes inconsequently or at will, but because their conceptual structure is based on the acceptance of moving parts – imagine a geometric wire sculpture which can be collapsed or expanded, and can have parts attached and separated in multiple combinations, but still maintains an inner logic. Or a matrix with multiple entries formed by entities and flows, which can be material or immaterial, natural or manmade, with an entry is controlled by sensorial and cultural filters.

This approach allows us to keep the core conceptual structure which is shared by space, place and territory, and still differentiate each of them. This is important because it avoids the common attempt to either define them as opposite concepts or as synonyms. Indeed, they are singular and complementary concepts. Furthermore, stressing that entities and flows are taken into this matrix only if screened by sensorial and cultural filters also helps us to avoid the reification of space, place and territory. Portions of space are not in themselves any of them: their definition depends on the way we perceive, understand and act in relation to entities and flows. They exist through negotiation.

Therefore, throughout the book, with essays ranging from how the meaning of darkness changes our understanding of space and mapping as a technique to create and enforce territories to the counterintuitive argument that airports, which are the perfect embodiment of global

Final remarks: spatial negotiations   163

exchanges, might be a place, or artistic interventions that challenge assented notions of space, I constantly diverted the discussion away from a presumably stable link between one spatial phenomenon and only one of these concepts.

In this book I have singled out cities to illustrate these matrixes. Cities, because they are densely populated, nodes of economic and cultural transactions, functioning through complex infrastructures, are privileged human settlements for discussing space, place and territory. By living in cities, our perception of spatial features changes. On the one hand, the entities and flows existing in cities are distinct and arguably more diverse than those existing in other settlements, and on the other hand living in cities changes our sensorial and cultural filters to a degree that we become unable to perceive some natural stimuli, and perspicacious in perceiving others.

However, I have also looked for examples on larger and smaller scales – from civilizational transformations and geopolitics to artistic interventions and dream spaces. The intention to broaden the range of examples was meant to demonstrate that each spatial phenomenon, event and intervention is the result of negotiations we as individuals and society establish between entities and flows screened by sensorial and cultural filters, regardless of the size of these phenomena. This makes spatial matrixes a conceptual device, and negotiation a methodological approach to perceiving, understanding and creating spaces, places and territories.

Index

Note: Locators in *italic* refer to figures

22@BCN, Barcelona 144–5

Agnew, John 29, 44, 54
airports 8, 33–4, 137–41, 143
Al-Qaeda 67–8
Anderson, Kay 42
Archigram 141–2
architecture 1, 7, 39–40, 91, 121, 131, 141; space design 28
artificial lights 91–3, 149
artworks 8–9, 150, *151*, 152–4, 155, 156
Ashcraft, Norman 45
astronomers 19, 21, 25, 27, 28, 65
astronomical space 19, 25–7, 28, 65
Augé, Marc 33, 71, 137

Bachelard, Gaston 38, 39, 75
Badie, Bertrand 52, 56
Barcelona 116, 144–5
Baudrillard, Jean 33, 57
Beacon Hill neighbourhood 35
Benjamin, Walter 31
Berlin Wall 8, 135–7, 157
biological filters 16, 18–19
blackouts 88–9, 149
borders 50, 52, 55, 102
boundaries 48–9, 50, 52, 55, 57, 156
Boylan Heights 104–5
brain activity 5, 80, 84–7, 94
Brasília 7, 117, *118*, 119–21, 122–7, 130, 134
Burri, René 126

Cage, John 93
Canada 15–16, 43–4, 66–7

Candlin, Fiona 87
Carnival 74
cartography 55, 56, 100, 103, 107–8, 109
Casey, Edward 2, 12, 30
Catholic Church 18, 45, 47, 48, 71, 72
Catholic territory 45, 47
caves 39–40
China 101, 116, 132
Chinatowns 42
Christianity 48, 71, 74
Christo (artist) 8–9, 150, 152, 153–4, 156
cities 29, 31–2, 116–17, 141–2, 144–5, 149, 161–2, 163; city 4–5, 34, 56; city plans 7–8, 130, 131–3
city plans 7–8, 130, 131–3
city-states 47–8, 49, 51
Cold War 67, 70
continental space 65
Cook, Peter 7, 141–2
Cooper, Becky 105
Costa, Lucio 117, 119, 120–1, 122, 123, 126
Cresswell, Tim 30, 39, 40, 42
cultural filters 7, 15–16, 18–21, 24–5, 28, 63–4, 79, 93–4, 162

darkness 6, 80, 87, 88–91, 93, 94, 162
Davis, Wade 37, 73
Deleuze, Gilles 48, 49
Derrida, Jacques 12
digital technologies 8, 99, 110, 134, 143

166 *Index*

Dogville (von Trier, 2003) 75–6
domesticity 39, 140, 141
domestic space 38–9, 75
domestic violence 38–9
dreams 14, 15, 16–18

ecological light pollution 92–3
Edgerton, Samuel 107
EEG (electroencephalography) 5, 80, 85–7
Einstein, Albert 25
Eisenman, Peter 150
Elden, Stuart 2, 12, 27, 33, 48, 53, 68
Elsinore castle, Denmark 42
Enigma of Kaspar Hauser, The (Herzog, 1974) 22
epistemological tools 6, 27, 30
Eudoxus 25, 27, 66
Europeans 53, 63, 65, 66, 68
European Union 64, 92
Evenson, Norman 121, 123

Ferrara, Lucrécia 30, 33, 56
First People, Canada 66–7
Flaubert, Gustave 23
Florence 105, *106*, 107
flows 12, 14, 18, 19–20, 21, 24–5, 149, 162
France 43, 53, 54, 116, 133
free runners *see* parkour (traceurs)

Gautherot, Marcel 125
global positioning system (GPS) 99–100
global space 8, 140, 141, 144
graffitti 136, 157
Greek city 47
Guattari, Félix 48, 49
Gulf cities 132
Guth, Alan 25, 27

Hall, Edward 15, 20, 21, 22, 23, 45, 46, 63
hearing 87, 88, 161–2
Heidegger, Martin 12, 40
Herbert, Jean-Loup 117
Herzog, Werner 22
Hillier, Bill 129–30
Hirt, Irène 17
Hoffman, Jeffrey 19, 23
home 37, 38–9, 41, 74
Horton, John 16

HubCab 111
Huntington, Samuel 70

indigenous peoples 15–16, 17, 66–7, 68, 162
infinite space 15
information and communication technologies 8, 109, 134, 141–3, 144, 145
innovation district 144–5
Inuit 15–16, 67, 162
Invisible Cities 110
Islamic culture 70
Islamic State 68

Jacobs, Jane 115, 116
Japan 20
Jeanne-Claude 8, 150, 152, 153–4
Jencks, Charles 150
Jerusalem 29, 71, 74
Jung, Carl 40–1

Khôra 11–12
Kim, Lina 126
Koolhaas, Rem 149–50
Kraftl, Peter 16
Kurds 56, 69

landscape 2, 20, 41, 102, 103, 154
land-use planning 7–8, 65, 82, 130–1
language 15–16, 24, 26, 28, 53, 100
Lau, Lisa 72
Le Corbusier 117, 130
Lefebvre, Henri 3, 14, 16, 18, 27, 33, 130
Leibniz, G.W. 12–13
light pollution 92–3
Lilley, Keith 29
linguistic structures 15–16
Lispector, Clarice 124
location 29–30, 71
Lynch, Kevin 20, 31, 35, 103–4

Maguire, Eleanor 84
Manhattan 34, 35–6, 105, 131–2, 133
mapmaking 100, 101, 102, 105, 107–8, 109–11
maps 6–7, 55, 63, 99–102, 104–5, 107–11; cities 6–7, 102, 103–4, 105, *106*, 107, 110, 111
Mapuche people 17
Marejko, Jan 15, 33

maritime space 65
Massey, Doreen 13, 38, 41, 42
matrices 63–4, 66, 76
McLuhan, Marshall 8, 23, 141
Mecca 36, 71, 74
Medellín, Colombia 134
Miller, Naomi 40, 105
Mitchell, William 134, 143
modernist city 7, 32, 119, 121,
   126–7, 130, 131; *see also* Brasília
modernization 82
modern space 33, 57
monuments 9, 151, 156–7, 158–9
Moses, Robert 115, 116
Muslims 36, 70, 74

national identity 51–2, 53, 54–5, 56
nation states 50, 52–5, 56, 57, 66–7,
   69–70, 101–2
Native Americans 66, 68
native languages 15–16
neighbourhoods 35, 36, 42
Newton, Isaac 12, 25, 26
New Urbanism 35
New York 34, 35–6, 92, 105, 111,
   115, 116, 157; Manhattan 34,
   35–6, 105, 131–2, 133
Nicoletti, Manfredi 39–40
Nicosia, Cyprus 129–30
Niemeyer, Oscar 117, 119, 120, 121,
   123
night 6, 87, 88, 89–91, 93, 94
nomads 48–9
non-places 8, 9, 33, 133, 137, 139,
   142
North Korea 51–2, 53, 67

odours *see* smells
olfactory memories 5, 80–1
oneiric space 14, 16–18, 27
Ottoman Empire 56, 69
outer space 23, 28, 67, 162

Paris 43, 116, 133; *Pont Neuf*
   wrapping 8–9, 153, 154
parkour (traceurs) 9, 155–6
patriarchal societies 72
Pavić, Milorad 17
perception 30, 31, 56; *see also* spatial
   perception
Perfume (Süskind, 1986) 22, 81–2
Perilous Night, The (Cage, 1944) 93
personal space 40–2

physical space 45, 55, 129, 144
Pit and the Pendulum, The
   (Poe, 1850) 22, 46–7, 87
place 1–4, 7, 29–30, 44–5, 63, 64, 71,
   74, 161; space 30, 33–4, 36, 43, 44,
   75, 76; territory 44, 51, 71–3
place construction 29–30, 33–4, 36–8,
   39–43, 44, 131
places 33, 75, 129, 143–4, 145
Plato 51
Poe, Edgar Allen 17, 22
Pont Neuf wrapping 8–9, 153, 154
Price, Joshua 38–9
printing press 57
projections 9, 157–8, 159
public lighting 6, 88, 90–2, 149

Quebec City 43–4

Real Time Rome 111
region 1–2
religious territories 45, 47, 48, 71,
   72–3, 74
representation 6, 23, 24, 26, 100,
   111
Romeo and Juliet (Shakespeare)
   49–50
Running Fence 152–3
Rybczynski, Witold 39, 140
Rykwert, Joseph 29

Sack, Robert 46
Santos, Milton 13–14
scents 20, 80, 81, 83
Scheflen, Albert 45
scientific mathematical space 15, 25
sensorial filters 7, 20–1, 22–3, 24–5,
   28, 79, 80, 94, 162
shamans 16
Shields, Rob 3, 13, 14, 26
Siegfried, André 20–1
sight 6, 20, 21–2, 23, 79, 87–8, 94
situationists 104
sleep 14, 15, 16–18, 19
slums 31, 56, 102
smells 5, 20–1, 22, 79, 80–4, 93–4,
   161
social groups 47, 66, 73
social space 14, 38–9, 81–2
social values 4, 36, 37, 41, 42, 73,
   161
Sophists 50–1
sounds 87, 88, 161–2

168 *Index*

space 1–6, 7, 12–14, 16–21, 63, 64–6, 149, 156, 161; place 30, 33–4, 36, 43, 44, 75, 76; territory 66–7, 76
space construction 11, 24–8, 44, 79, 131–2
space syntax 130
spatial experience 5, 19, 31, 80, 85–7, 129
spatial matrices 2, 4, 9, 64, 65, 66, 68, 149, 161, 163
spatial perception 6, 21–3, 30–1, 33, 66, 80, 94, 161–2, 163
spatial phenomena 2, 3, 4, 9, 25, 63, 64, 161, 163
spatial rules 33, 47, 102–3, 130–1, 154–5
spatial stimuli 84–5
spatial systems 18, 21–2, 24, 25, 27
state sovereignty 53–4
Stein, Gertrude 124
Surrounded Islands 150, *151*, 152
symbols 9, 54, 55, 156–7, 158–9

taxi drivers 84
technological development 57, 110, 142
technological fatalism 150
technological instruments 23–4, 65
technologies 23–4, 67, 80, 134
telecommunications 134, 141, 142
telescopes 23
territoriality 45, 46, 52, 56, 68–9
territorial matrices 67, 68, 69–71
territorial rules 47, 51, 53, 54, 156
territorial technology 6, 100, 101, 102
territorial units 66, 67–71
territory 1–4, 7, 47–8, 49, 50, 51–6, 57, 63, 64, 156–7, 161; place 44, 51, 71–3; space 66–7, 76
territory construction 44, 45–6, 47, 56–7, 67–71, 131
Timaeus 11–12

Tolaas, Sissel 21, 82–3
touch 79, 87
tourist guides 43
traceurs *see* parkour (traceurs)
travelling 24, 43, 90, 99; *see also* airports
Tuan, Yi-Fu 2, 16, 23, 34, 36, *55*

Umbanda 72–3, 75
ummah 70
United States 48, 67, 73, 89, 91–2; *see also* New York
universe 25–6
urban design 7–8, 32, 116, 132
urban infrastructures 102, 133, 134, 149, 154–5
urbanity 117, 127, 132, 141–2, 144, 145
urbanization 132, 134
urban planning 32, 102, 116, 130–3
urban reconstruction 115, 116
urban space 8, 32, 65, 116, 130–4, 141–2, 149, 154–5, 159–60

Vaughan, Laura 129–30
Virilio, Paul 142
virtual reality 85
vision *see* sight

Walser, Robert 14
weaving 133, 134
Wesely, Michael 126
Whyte, William 32
Wodiczko, Krzysztof 8, 157–8, 159
women 38–9, 72
Wood, Denis 104–5
Woods, Lebbeus 136–7
Wrapped Reichstag 153–4
wrapping interventions 150, *151*, 152, 153–4, 156

zoning 102–3, 130